SCIENCE
HORIZONS

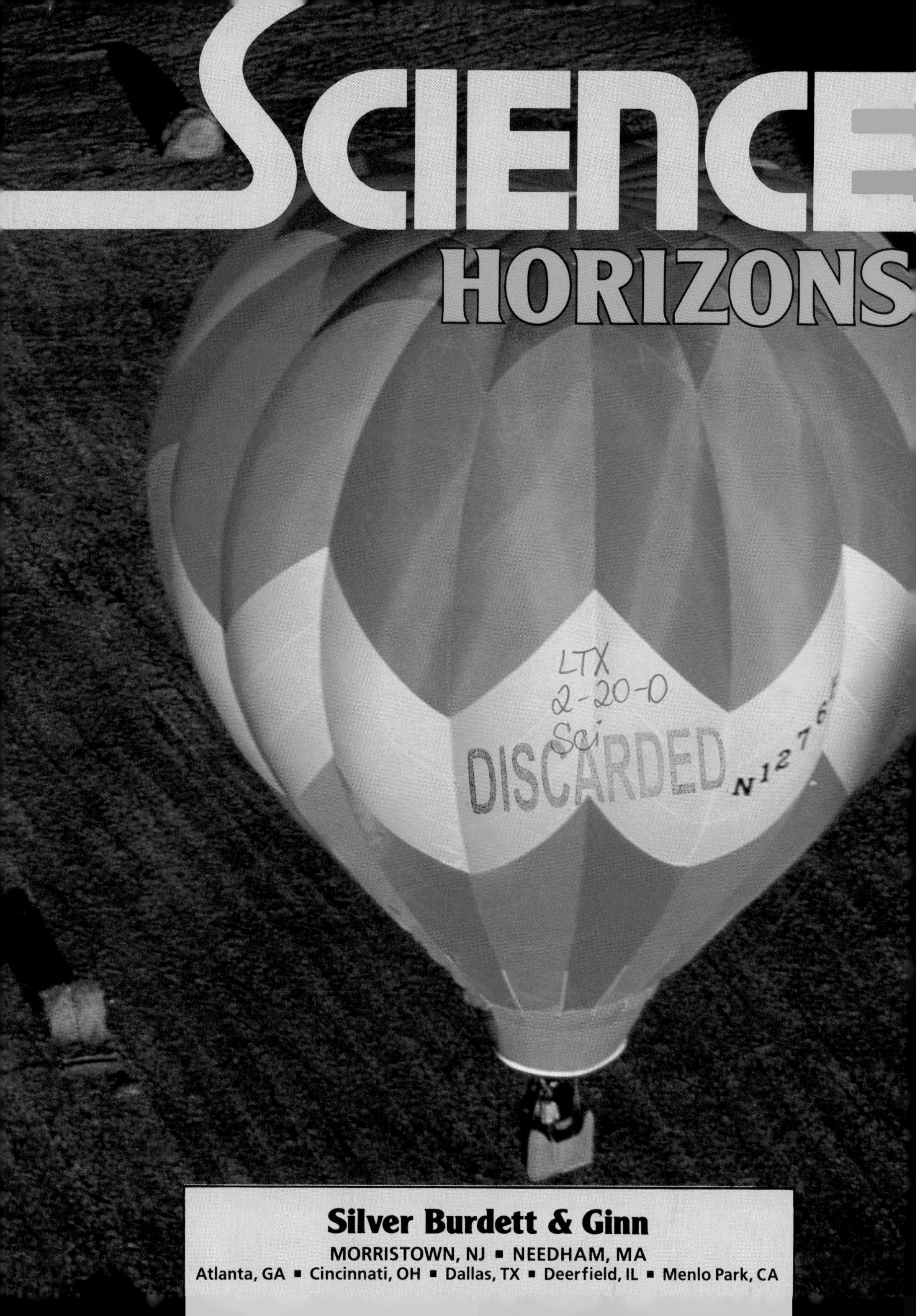

LTX
2-20-0
Sci
DISCARDED N1276

Silver Burdett & Ginn

MORRISTOWN, NJ ▪ NEEDHAM, MA

Atlanta, GA ▪ Cincinnati, OH ▪ Dallas, TX ▪ Deerfield, IL ▪ Menlo Park, CA

SCIENCE HORIZONS

George G. Mallinson
Distinguished Professor
of Science Education
Western Michigan University

Jacqueline B. Mallinson
Associate Professor of Science
Western Michigan University

Linda Froschauer
Science Senior Teacher
Central Middle School
Greenwich, Connecticut

James A. Harris
Principal, D.C. Everest
Area School District
Schofield, Wisconsin

Melanie C. Lewis
Professor, Department of Biology
Southwest Texas State University
San Marcos, Texas

Catherine Valentino
Former Director of Instruction
North Kingstown School Department
North Kingstown, Rhode Island

Dedicated with love
to our colleague, teacher, and friend
Denny McMains
whose talent and courage were
the inspiration for Science Horizons

Acknowledgments appear on pages 330–332, which constitute an extension of this copyright page.

Dear Boys and Girls,

Welcome to the world of science. This book will help you understand your world. You will discover new ways to look at things. You will learn new ways to think. This year you will ask many questions. And on your own you will find the answers. You will become good problem solvers.

What things do you wonder about? Do you wonder about sounds? This year you will make your own sound maker. Do you wonder about animals of long ago? You will meet other people who wonder too. They make models of dinosaurs. This year you will make your own dinosaur models.

Your world is filled with wonders. And science is a part of everything you do. So, turn the page to find out what lies ahead. We wish you an exciting year. Have fun!

Your friends,
The Authors

Contents

Unit One
Life Science

Unit Two
Physical Science

Unit Three
Earth Science

Unit Four
Human Body

Return of the Dinosaurs

Did you ever wonder what dinosaurs were like? Many people wonder about dinosaurs. Dinosaurs lived long ago. No one has ever seen a living dinosaur.

What sounds did dinosaurs make?
How did they move? What colors were
they? Suppose you could stand next to a
dinosaur. How would you feel? There is
one way for you to find out.

These people make models of dinosaurs. They are part of a special team. The team is made up of scientists, artists, and others. They want the models to look, sound, and move like real dinosaurs. They want people to come to see the models.

How do the team members find out about dinosaurs? First they search for clues about what dinosaurs looked like. They look at dinosaur bones and teeth. They use these clues to learn what a whole dinosaur might have looked like.

The team also looks at pictures of dinosaur footprints. Footprints give clues about the size and weight of a dinosaur. Footprints also can show how the animal moved.

The artists make drawings of what they think the dinosaurs looked like. The scientists check the drawings. They make sure the drawings match the way the dinosaur bones fit together.

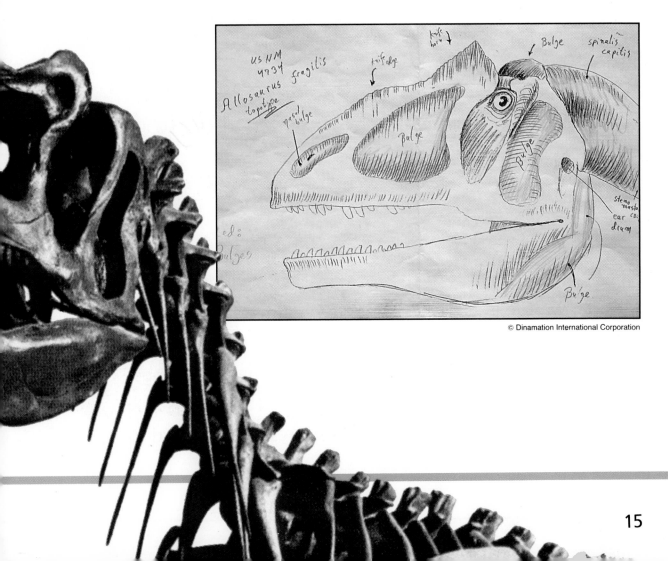

Skills

Learning from pictures

It takes many skills to make a dinosaur model. You have many skills. Reading numbers and adding them are skills. You will use these and many other skills in science.

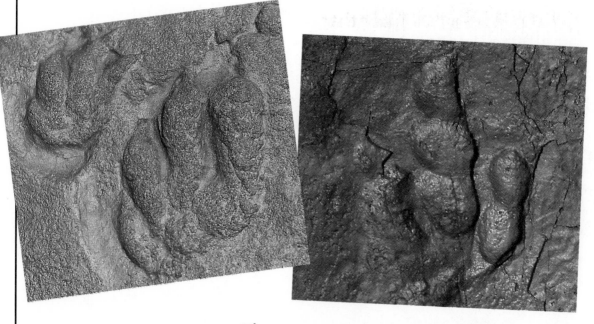

The team made drawings. The drawings helped team members figure out how dinosaurs might have looked. Your science book has many drawings and pictures. You can learn things from drawings and pictures that are hard to learn from words.

Practice

1. Look at the drawings of dinosaur footprints.

2. Write something about each footprint that you can learn by looking at the drawings. Look at the number of toes. Think about the size of the foot that made the footprint. Think about the shape of the foot.

3. Choose one drawing of a footprint. Make a drawing of a dinosaur foot that could have made that footprint.

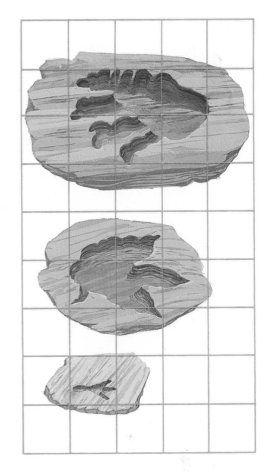

Apply

Look at this picture of a dinosaur foot. Draw what its footprint might look like.

The team members must find out
all they can about each dinosaur. They
must learn if it walked on two legs or
four legs. They need to find out the size
of each body part. Did the dinosaur have
claws on its feet? How big was its
mouth? Did it have sharp teeth?

Next the team makes a small dinosaur model. The small model is made from clay. The clay model is very real-looking. The team looks carefully at the model. They want to be sure it matches what they learned about the dinosaur.

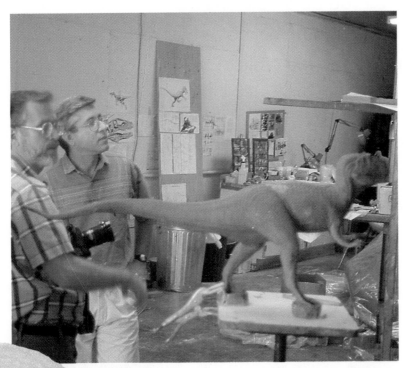

Explore Together

How can you make a dinosaur model?

Many people worked as a team to build dinosaur models. When you do an **Explore Together** activity you will also be part of a team. Working together makes the job easier. Each team member has a job to do.

The Planner gets the things you need. The Leader uses the things. The Helper helps the Leader. The Writer writes what happens or makes a drawing. The Reporter tells the class what the group did. All means that every group member helps.

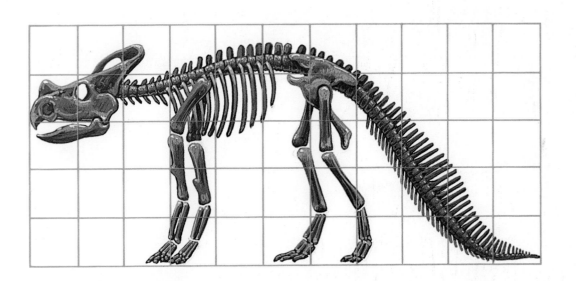

You need

Planner tracing paper • marker • paste • colored paper • scissors • clay

What to do

Writer 1. Place tracing paper on the drawing of the dinosaur skeleton. Trace the outline of the dinosaur skeleton.

Helper 2. Paste the tracing onto a piece of colored paper. Use scissors to cut out the outline. **Be careful!** Scissors can cut you.

All 3. Study the skeleton. Tell the Leader how the dinosaur might have looked.

Leader 4. Use the clay to make a model of the dinosaur.

What did you find out?

Writer, All 1. Does the model look as you think it should?

Reporter 2. Tell your class about your model.

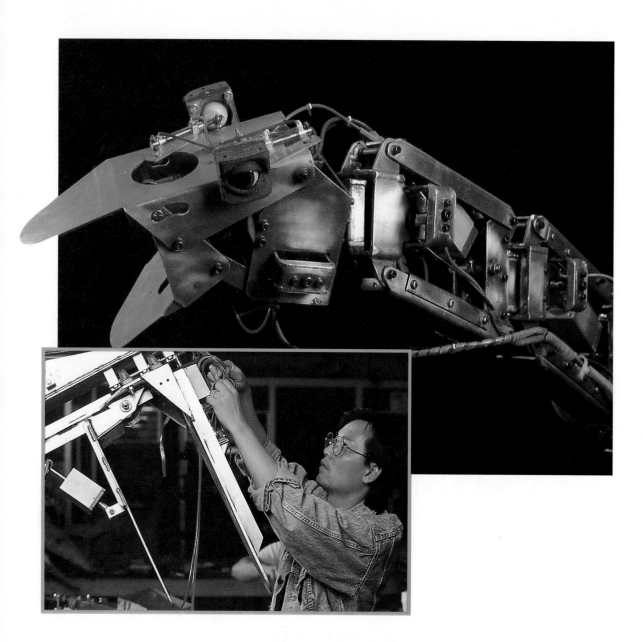

Now the team is ready to make their dinosaur. First they make bones for the dinosaur. The bones are made from metal. The metal bones are joined together. They will help to make the model move like a real dinosaur.

The metal bones are moved by motors and tubes. The motors pump air through the tubes. The air makes the head, eyes, and tail move. The eyes can blink and the tail can wave back and forth.

The team members are almost done with their dinosaur. But they still have one more problem to solve. What should the skin look like? How will they make it?

Problem Solving

A Big Cover-up

ACTIVITY

When you solve problems you find answers to questions. There are four steps.

THINK about the problem.

PLAN how you should solve the problem.

Get the things you need and then

DO what you planned.

SHARE what you did.

The team members want the skin of their model to look real. But they are not sure how it should look. You can help them solve the problem.

What should the dinosaur skin look like?

Think   Think about animals living today. Which
ones might have skin that is like dinosaur
skin?

Plan   Use flat pieces of clay as skin. Think how
you want the skin to look. What could
you press into the clay to make the skin
look that way?

Do   Get the things you need. Follow your plan
to make the clay look like dinosaur skin.

Share   Show others your dinosaur skin. Tell how
you made it.

The team members decide on the kind of skin their dinosaur should have. Then they must choose colors to paint the skin. They look at animals of today for ideas.

Snakes and lizards of today are more like dinosaurs than other animals are. Some lizards are orange. Others are green. Some snakes have stripes. Others have spots. What colors do you think dinosaurs were? Team members painted spots on their model.

SCIENCE
HORIZONS

LIFE SCIENCE

Chapter 1

Grouping Animals

On your mark. Get set. Leap frog!
The race is on. Each frog must jump
three times. Judges measure each jump.
Then they add the jumps together.

One frog, named Rosie the Ribiter,
jumped the farthest. Her jumps added
up to 6 meters, or as long as a school bus.

Scientists also measure how far frogs can jump. They want to know which frogs jump farthest and fastest. Scientists learn all they can about many different animals.

In this chapter you will learn about groups of animals. Frogs are in one group. You will also learn about other groups.

1. How can animals be grouped?

Words to Know
body covering

Getting Started Make a list of animals that can be seen in a zoo. How can you group them?

Birds! Tigers! Snakes! There are many kinds of animals. Animals that are alike in some way are put in the same group. You might group animals by their sizes or shapes. Or you might group them by where they live.

◀Flamingo

▼Tiger

One way scientists group animals is by how their young form. Some animals, such as dogs, have young that are born live. Others, such as frogs, lay eggs.

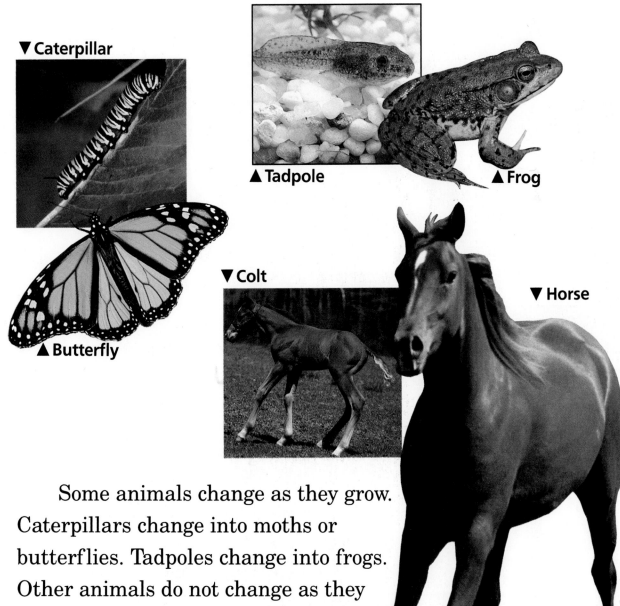

▼ Caterpillar

▲ Tadpole

▲ Frog

▲ Butterfly

▼ Colt

▼ Horse

Some animals change as they grow. Caterpillars change into moths or butterflies. Tadpoles change into frogs. Other animals do not change as they grow. Point to the baby animal that looks like its parent.

Another way scientists group animals is by body covering. The **body covering** of an animal helps protect it. What kind of animal has feathers? Scales, fur, and shells are other kinds of body coverings. What animals have these coverings?

▲ Ducklings

▲ Goldfish

▲ Rabbit

▲ Box turtle

Lesson Review

1. What are some ways that animals can be grouped?
2. What are two ways that the young of animals form?

Think! How could you group the animals in your neighborhood?

ACTIVITY

Explore Together
How can you group animals?

You need

Planner scissors • old magazines • glue • colored paper

What to do

All 1. Cut out many pictures of animals. **Be careful!** Scissors can cut you.

Helper 2. Glue each picture on colored paper.

All 3. Think of ways to group the animals.

Writer 4. Write down the ideas.

Leader 5. Use the list of ideas to sort the animal pictures into groups.

What did you find out?

All, Writer 1. What different ways did you group the animals?

Reporter 2. Share what you found out with the class.

2. How are raccoons and robins different?

Getting Started   Some raccoons get food from garbage cans. Robins peck for worms. What else do you know about raccoons and robins?

▲ Bat

These baby raccoons are drinking milk. Raccoons are mammals. A **mammal** is an animal that gets milk from its mother's body. All the animals on these pages are mammals. What can you tell about each one?

Most mammals have fur or hair. Most of them have young that are born live. All baby mammals drink milk from their mother. All mammals breathe with lungs.

Mammals are many sizes. Whales are large mammals. Mice are small mammals. Some mammals live in water, but most of them live on land. What other mammals can you name?

Orangutan ▲

▲ Killer whales

▲ Robins

These baby robins are waiting for their food. A parent is getting worms for them to eat. Robins belong to a group of animals called birds.

A **bird** is an animal that has wings and a beak. Birds are the only animals that have feathers. All birds lay eggs. Most birds make nests for their eggs.

Canada ▶
goose

You can look for birds in many places. Some birds, such as robins, make their nests in trees. Other birds, such as geese, make their nests on the ground.

Some birds, such as ducks, spend a lot of time in water. Some birds spend a lot of time on land. Other birds spend a lot of time flying in the air. How are all of the birds in these pictures alike? How are they different?

▲ Mallard duck nest

▲ Ring-billed gull

▼ Mallard duck with ducklings

◄ Brown pelican

39

Bats are animals that look like birds. A bat can fly. But it does not have feathers. It does not lay eggs. A bat is not a bird. A bat is a mammal.

Not all birds can fly. These penguins are birds that cannot fly. Their wings are used for swimming.

◀ **Bats**

▲ **Penguins**

Lesson Review

1. What is a mammal?
2. What is a bird?

Think! Why is flying helpful to birds?

Skills

Finding words that tell about things

You see a bird. You see that the bird is blue. You see that the bird is also small. The words "blue" and "small" can tell about the bird.

Practice

1. Look at the horses. You can see that one is black. The word "black" tells about that horse.
2. What else can you say to tell about some of the horses?
3. What can you say to tell about all of the horses?

Apply

Look at the hens. What can you say to tell about the hens?

3. How are goldfish and snails different?

Words to Know
fish
mollusk

Getting Started Pretend you have a large bowl of fresh water. What animals could you keep alive in it?

These goldfish are looking for food. Goldfish are fish. **Fish** are animals that live and breathe under water. Most fish are covered with scales. Most fish have fins. What do fish use their fins for?

▲ Fish breathe with gills.

scales

fins

gills

Have you ever wondered how fish breathe? Fish do not have lungs as mammals do. Most fish breathe through slits in the sides of their head. These slits are called gills.

▼ Fish eggs

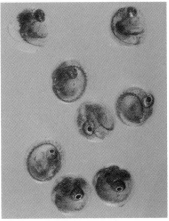

Most fish hatch from soft eggs. Some fish, such as guppies, have live young. Baby fish look just like their parents.

Like fish, some snails live in water. Snails are mollusks. A **mollusk** is an animal with a soft body. A snail has a hard shell covering its body. Snails do not have fins or legs. They move around on one big, slimy foot. Like some fish, snails lay eggs. How would you group these snails?

▲ Many kinds of snails

Lesson Review

1. What is a fish?
2. What are some differences between a fish and a snail?

Think! In what ways does having a hard shell help a snail?

Explore

How well do snails see?

Some scientists think that snails cannot see shapes. They think that snails can only see brightness and darkness. These glasses will let you see like a snail.

You need

glue • frame for snail glasses • posterboard • scissors • tape • wax paper

What to do

1. Glue the frame for snail glasses to posterboard.
2. Cut out the frames. **Be careful!** Scissors can cut you.
3. Cut holes where the glass would be.
4. Tape wax paper over each hole.
5. Put the glasses on.

What did you find out?

How did things look through the snail glasses?

4. How are garter snakes and bullfrogs different?

Words to Know

reptile
amphibian

Getting Started   What do you think the skin of this garter snake feels like?

Garter snake▶

Did you ever wish you had a zoo at your home? Read about a boy and girl who made their own zoo in **The Backyard Zoo** in Horizons Plus.

A garter snake is a reptile. A **reptile** is an animal that has scaly skin. The cool, dry skin of a snake feels smooth when you rub it one way. It feels rough when you rub it the other way. But do not touch a snake. It might bite.

Most reptiles lay eggs that have thick shells. They lay their eggs on land. Some reptiles, such as the garter snake, are born live. Baby reptiles look like their parents.

▲ Turtle hatching

Alligators and turtles are also reptiles. They spend a lot of time in water. But they must poke their heads out to breathe. That is because reptiles breathe with lungs, not with gills.

◀ River turtle

▲ Alligators

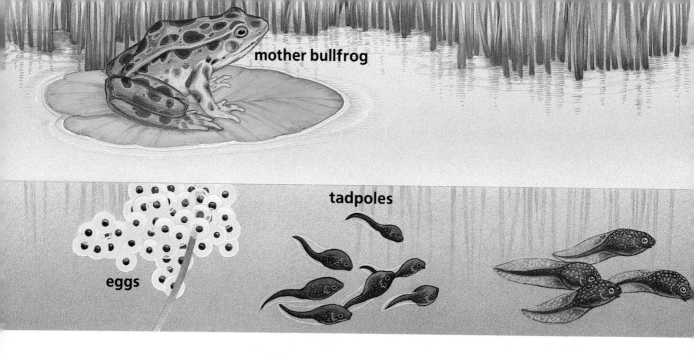

mother bullfrog

eggs

tadpoles

You read about frogs on pages 30 and 31. These tadpoles are changing to frogs. Frogs are amphibians. An **amphibian** is an animal that lives part of its life in water and part on land. It has thin, wet skin. Unlike a reptile, a baby amphibian does not look like its parents. Its body changes as it grows. Newts and toads are amphibians.

▼ Newt

Toad ▶

young frog

tadpoles grow legs

A mother bullfrog lays many eggs in water. Tadpoles hatch from these eggs. Tadpoles breathe with gills. What other animals breathe with gills?

▼ Bullfrog

As tadpoles grow, their bodies change. They grow legs, and their tails get shorter. As tadpoles grow into frogs, their gills close up. They grow lungs. They have become frogs. Frogs can breathe in the air.

Lesson Review ━━━━━━

1. What is a reptile?

2. How does a bullfrog change as it grows?

Think! How are mammals and amphibians alike? How are they different?

5. How are grasshoppers and spiders different?

Getting Started Have you ever seen a grasshopper close up? What does it look like?

grasshopper

A grasshopper is an insect. An **insect** is an animal with six legs. The body of an insect has a hard covering. It is something like your fingernails. There are many kinds of insects. What can you tell about the legs of these insects?

beetle

honeybee

praying mantis

ladybug

All insects lay eggs. This grasshopper lays its eggs underground. The baby grasshoppers look like their parents. As they get older, they just get bigger.

grasshopper laying eggs   baby grasshopper

young grasshopper

Moths are insects, too. Baby moths are called caterpillars. They do not look like their parents. Their bodies change as they grow. How is this caterpillar different from its parent?

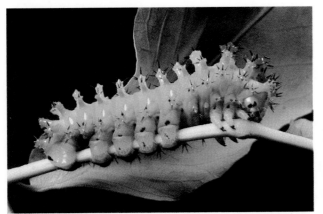

▲ Caterpillar

▲ Moth

▲ Garden spider

▼ Spiders hatching

This garden spider is spinning a web. A **spider** is an animal with eight legs. The body of a spider has a hard covering like that of an insect. There are many kinds of spiders. They lay eggs as insects do. Baby spiders look like their parents.

Most spiders eat by sucking juice out of insects. Do you know how they catch insects? Most spiders build webs. The webs are made out of sticky silk thread. This thread comes out of a spider's body. Insects stick to the web. Then the spider bites the insects. Never touch a spider. It might bite you.

▲ Tarantula

▼ Spider eating a grasshopper

▲ Black widow spider

Lesson Review

1. What is an insect?
2. What is a spider?

Think! How are insects and spiders alike? How are they different?

Problem Solving
You Can Say That Again!

Crickets are insects. Have you ever heard crickets chirping? Think about the sounds a cricket makes. Did you hear them in winter or summer? What time of day was it? Suppose you wanted to make a cricket chirp.

What might cause a cricket to chirp more?

Think of a plan. Try to make a cricket chirp as many times in 5 minutes as you can. Be careful not to hurt the cricket. Be sure to wash your hands when finished.

Chapter Connections

Draw the word map on a paper. Find pictures to cut and paste in the blue shapes of your word map.

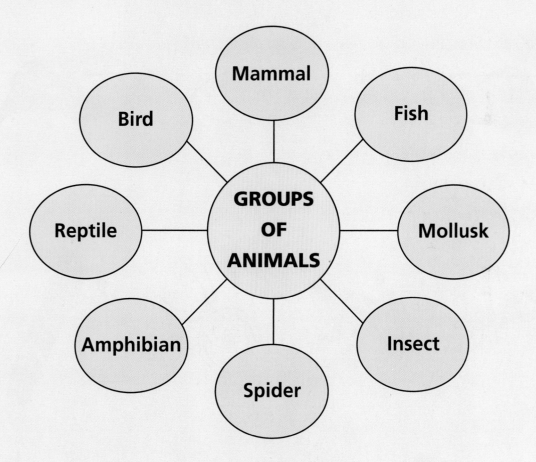

Writing About Science • Describe

Draw a picture of an animal baby. Write a sentence about where the baby lives.

Science Words

Match each word with a picture.

amphibian   bird   body covering   fish   insect
mammal   mollusk   reptile   spider

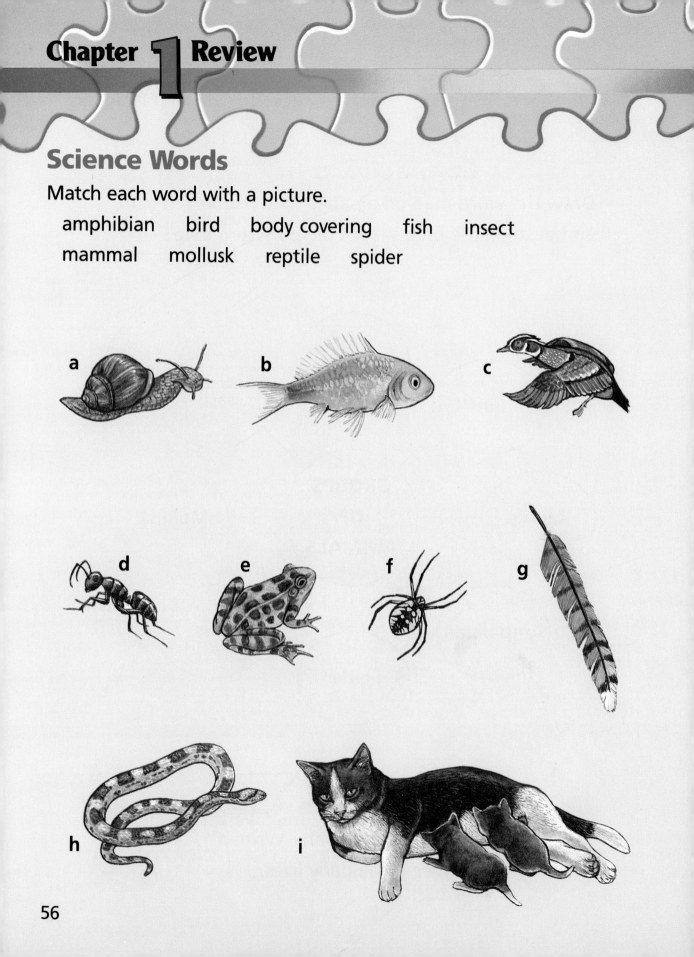

a

b

c

d

e

f

g

h

i

Science Ideas

Which facts are true for each animal? You may use each fact more than once.

1. amphibian	**a.**	Has feathers and wings
2. bird	**b.**	Has eight legs
3. fish	**c.**	Has six legs
4. insect	**d.**	Has scales
5. mammal	**e.**	Has a soft body
6. mollusk	**f.**	Has fur or hair
7. reptile	**g.**	Breathes with gills
8. spider	**h.**	Has a hard outer covering
	i.	Babies drink milk from the mother's body

Applying Science Ideas

Pretend you have a fish tank. You put two tadpoles into it. What changes will you need to make as the tadpoles grow?

Using Science Skills

Look at the raccoons on page 36. What words tell about the raccoons?

2

Growing Plants

Have you ever walked through a field of wildflowers? In some parts of the country, there are few wildflowers now. People raised cattle or built houses where the wildflowers once grew.

With too little space, wildflowers could die out. But many people are trying to save them. Some people grow wildflowers in their garden. Wildflowers are easy to grow because they need little care.

In this chapter you will learn about plants and how they grow. You will find out how they make seeds.

1. How do plants form seeds?

Words to Know
cones
flowers
pollen

Getting Started Look at the inside of a fruit. What do you see?

Many plants form seeds. Some plants form seeds as big as soccerballs. Other plants form very tiny seeds. How can you group seeds?

You may have wondered where seeds come from. Some plants have **cones**. Seeds form inside the cones. Other plants have **flowers**. Many wildflowers are shown on pages 58 and 59. Seeds form inside the flowers.

▲ Pine cone and seeds

How do seeds form? **Pollen** is made by one part of a flower. Some pollen looks like bits of yellow dust.

Insects and birds often pick up pollen on their bodies. They carry it from flower to flower. Point to the pollen on the bee. The wind also blows pollen. When pollen lands on a flower of the same kind, seeds may form.

Clint never dreamed he would have to work so hard to win first prize. Read about it in **The Blue Ribbon Season** in Horizons Plus.

Look at the pictures. They show
how seeds form. First a flower grows on
the plant. Tiny eggs are in the flower.
These eggs need pollen in order to grow
into seeds.

▼ **Part of flower with seeds**

▲ **Flower**

When the pollen reaches the eggs, the seeds start to form. A tiny plant begins to grow inside each seed. The part of the flower that holds the seeds grows into a fruit. That is why you often find seeds inside fruit.

▼ Young fruit

▲ Fruit

Lesson Review

1. In what part of a plant are seeds formed?
2. Tell how a seed forms in a flower.

Think! Why are bees important to plants?

How can a super carrot help people?

Why are carrots good for you? They have carotene in them. Lots of foods have this. In your body it turns into vitamin A. Vitamin A is good for your eyes. It helps you stay well.

Some people do not get enough carotene. So these people do not have much vitamin A. Children who do not have enough vitamin A get sick often. They can also go blind.

A group of scientists have grown a super carrot. They call it Beta III. It has more carotene than a normal carrot. It tastes sweeter, too. Children who eat it may get sick less often than children who do not.

The scientists want to make Beta III taste even better. They also want to make it easy for farmers to grow. But Beta III plants can become unhealthy. The scientists are now looking for ways to keep them healthy while they grow.

Thinking about it

1. What makes a food good for you?

2. Is Beta III better than a normal carrot? Why or why not?

3. What is one problem with Beta III?

Using what you learned

The foods in the pictures all have carotene. What do you like or dislike about these foods?

tomatoes

blueberries

orange

corn

2. How are seeds scattered?

Getting Started Have you ever planted a seed? How did you take care of it?

Seeds are scattered in many ways. Sometimes the wind scatters seeds. Some seeds, such as maple seeds, look like they have wings. The seeds spin through the air. Other seeds are light and puffy. They can float through the air. What things do these seeds make you think of?

▲ Pine cone with seeds in water

66

▲ Seeds on squirrel

Some seeds are also scattered by animals. Some seeds stick to the fur of animals. What happens when these seeds fall off an animal?

Some seeds can float. They may be scattered by water. Other seeds are shot into the air. This happens when the pod that holds them dries up and bursts. How does this scatter seeds?

▲ Seed pod bursting

▲ Seeds in sun

▲ Seeds in shade

▲ Seeds on road

Some plants form many seeds. Then the seeds are scattered. They land in many different places. But not all the seeds will grow. What does a seed need to begin growing? It must have air, water, and warmth. In which place shown does a seed have the best chance of growing?

Lesson Review

1. How are seeds scattered by wind?
2. How do animals scatter seeds?

Think! How do people scatter seeds?

Problem Solving

All Aboard the Seed Express!

Pretend you are a scientist. You are trying to think of a way to scatter a seed. The seed is shown at the right.

How can this seed be scattered?

Invent a way for this seed to be scattered. Will the seed move in the air, on the water, or on an animal? Can your seed be scattered in more than one way?

3. How do seeds grow?

Words to Know
seed coat
sprout

Getting Started Look at the package of seeds. Why are the seeds not growing?

stored food

tiny plant

seed coat

Did you ever feel a seed? How did it feel? The hard covering of a seed is the **seed coat**. It protects the seed. Inside the seed coat is a tiny plant. Around the tiny plant is stored food. The tiny plant uses the food to begin growing.

You learned that seeds start to grow when they have air, water, and warmth. First, the seed coat splits open. Then the seed begins to **sprout**. This means that the tiny plant inside the seed breaks through the seed coat.

As it grows, the tiny plant uses the stored food in the seed. The small root grows down into the soil. Then the tiny plant grows up through the soil. A new plant is formed.

▲ Pea plant

As the plant grows, it needs air, light, and warmth. It also needs food, soil, and water. Plants make their own food. The food is used for energy.

A plant also needs space to grow. The plant gets bigger. It forms flowers. Seeds form inside each flower. These peas are seeds. Soon the seeds will be scattered. What will happen next?

▲ Peas in pea pod

Lesson Review

1. What is one way that a seed changes as it grows?
2. What do seeds need to grow?
3. What do plants need to grow?

Think! Plants need light to make food. Why do seeds not need light?

Skills

Finding out how plants are alike

To see how plants are alike, you can look at parts of the plants. A maple tree has green leaves in summer. That is a way it is like some other plants.

Practice

1. The pictures show two tree branches in winter. One has leaves. What does the other one look like?

2. List ways in which the branches are alike. How could you tell the trees apart?

▲ Maple

▲ Holly

Apply

Look at the two kinds of bean seeds. What are some words that describe each seed? How are the seeds alike? How are they different?

▲ Pinto bean   ▲ Lima bean

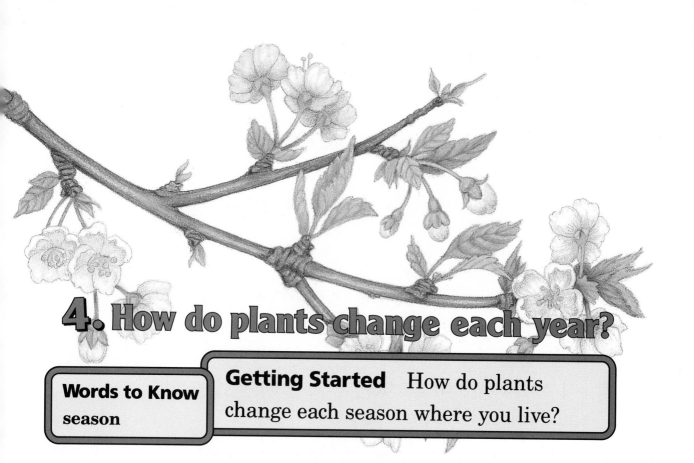

4. How do plants change each year?

Words to Know
season

Getting Started How do plants change each season where you live?

Plants change each season. A **season** is a time of year. Spring, summer, fall, and winter are the seasons. Many plants grow only part of the year. In some places, half of the year may be very dry. The other half of the year may be very wet. Other places have four different seasons. What are the seasons like where you live?

In spring the weather is warm. It rains on some days. Many seeds sprout. Leaves begin to grow on some trees.

▲ Seed sprouts

74

By summer the weather is very warm. Many small plants are fully grown. Flowers are formed. The leaves on many trees are large and green.

▼ Summer

By the end of summer, fruits and vegetables are ripe. They are ready to be picked. Flowers may start to dry up. The seeds have formed.

▲ Picking vegetables

In fall the weather becomes cooler. Leaves begin to change color. They may be red, yellow, or orange. These colored leaves will soon dry up and fall off the trees. Many seeds are scattered in the fall. What can you tell about the trees in the picture?

▼ Fall

Winter is a time when many plants stop growing. In some places the weather turns cold. Many trees lose their leaves. Many flowers are gone. In some places it snows. What is winter like where you live?

▲ Winter

Lesson Review

1. How do some plants change in the spring and summer?
2. In which season do many plants stop growing?

Think! Some trees may look dead in the winter. How do you know they are not dead?

Explore

ACTIVITY

What do seeds need in spring to start to grow?

Some people plant seeds in a garden. The seeds grow in the spring.

You need

4 paper towels • 4 resealable plastic bags • 16 lima bean seeds • water • refrigerator

What to do

1. Place a paper towel and four lima bean seeds in each of four plastic bags.
2. Add water to wet the beans in two of the bags.
3. Label the bags.
4. Place the bags marked "Cold" in the refrigerator. Place the bags marked "Warm" in a warm place.
5. Observe the seeds for 5 days.

What did you find out?

1. Which bag of seeds began to grow?
2. What do seeds need to start growing?

Chapter Connections

Draw pictures of what happens to plants each season where you live. Use the word map to help you.

GROWING PLANTS

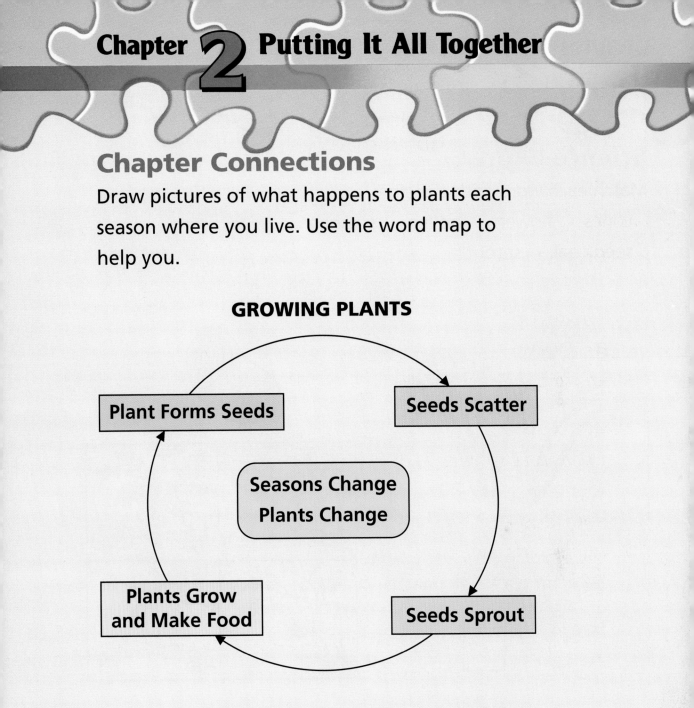

Plant Forms Seeds

Seeds Scatter

Seasons Change
Plants Change

Plants Grow
and Make Food

Seeds Sprout

Writing About Science • Imagine

Suppose you plant a pumpkin seed in early spring. Draw a picture to show what happens to your pumpkin plant each season. Write a sentence for each picture.

Science Words

Match each word with a picture.

cones   flowers   pollen   seasons

seed coat   sprout

a

b
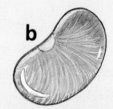

c
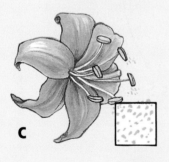

d

e

f
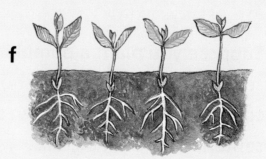

Science Ideas

1. What number shows where seeds form on the rosebush?
2. What are two ways that seeds can be scattered?
3. Name three things that seeds need in order to grow.
4. What happens to the seed coat as a seed sprouts?
5. Name five things that plants need in order to grow.
6. During which season are many seeds scattered?

Applying Science Ideas

Why do scientists want to make Beta III carrots taste better?

Using Science Skills

Look at the two kinds of seeds. How are they alike? How are they different?

Chapter 3

Living Things of Long Ago

Dinosaur eggs were laid long ago. Now scientists dig to find them. Eggs are found in some nests. There are bones of baby dinosaurs in other nests. The nests have food in them, too.

Scientists used to think mother dinosaurs did not take care of their young. But these nests give scientists a new idea about that. Maybe some dinosaurs <u>did</u> care for their young. Maybe the mother dinosaurs brought food to the babies in the nest.

In this chapter you will learn more about how scientists study dinosaurs. You will also learn what may have caused all the dinosaurs to die.

1. What animals lived long ago?

Words to Know
dinosaurs
plant eaters
meat eaters

Getting Started Look at the painting. What kinds of living things do you see?

Pretend you can go back in time. It is millions of years ago. Look around. There are no people on the earth. But there are plants and animals. Some of these animals of long ago are **dinosaurs**.

Many dinosaurs lived where it was warm and wet. Others lived where it was cool and dry. But all dinosaurs lived on land. They could not fly. They could not live under water. Which of these animals are dinosaurs? Which animals are not dinosaurs?

Did you ever want to know what it was like to find a dinosaur bone? Find out about a boy who found one in **Dinosaur Hunting** in Horizons Plus.

There were many kinds of dinosaurs. Some were taller than a giraffe. Others were the size of a chicken.

Scientists used to think all dinosaurs were dull in color. Now they think that some dinosaurs were brightly colored. Some dinosaurs may even have had spots or stripes like some snakes.

Most dinosaurs were **plant eaters**.
They ate only plants. Many plant eaters
were very tall. They could eat leaves
from the tops of trees. Plant eaters had
short, flat teeth.

▼ Plant eaters

Some dinosaurs were **meat eaters**. They ate other animals. They hunted slow or weak animals. Meat eaters had sharp, pointed teeth. Some had teeth that were longer than your hand. What are these meat eaters doing?

▲ Meat eaters

Lesson Review

1. What are two ways that dinosaurs could not move about?
2. In what ways did dinosaurs look different from one another?
3. How were the teeth of meat eaters different from the teeth of plant eaters?

Think! Why did the meat eaters hunt slow or weak animals?

Explore Together

What shape of teeth is good for chewing plants?

You need

Planner   2 tree leaves • 2 small wooden blocks • timer • 2 golf tees • cereal

What to do

Leader **1.** Pretend the blocks are flat teeth. Grind the leaf between two blocks for 1 minute.

Helper **2.** Time the Leader.

Writer **3.** Draw how the leaf changed.

Leader **4.** Pretend the golf tees are pointed teeth. Grind the second leaf for 1 minute.

Helper **5.** Time the Leader.

Writer **6.** Draw how the leaf changed.

All **7.** Repeat steps **1** through **6** using the cereal.

What did you find out?

All, Writer **1.** What can the teeth models do best?

Reporter **2.** Share your results with the class.

2. What happened to the dinosaurs?

Words to Know
extinct

Getting Started Think of your favorite kinds of animals. What would you miss most if they were no longer living?

Millions of years went by. Then the dinosaurs became **extinct**. That means that all the dinosaurs died. There are no more of them. Extinct animals can never return. That is why there are no dinosaurs today.

Why did the dinosaurs become extinct? No one knows for sure. People do know that the earth slowly changed. Some wet places became dry. Some warm places became cold.

Here is one idea. The dinosaurs did not have feathers or fur to keep them warm. Maybe they could not live in the cold. The animals shown here could keep warm. So they lived.

Here is another idea. Some scientists think a huge rock from space hit the earth. It made a lot of dust fly into the air. The dust blocked the light from the sun. The earth became cold and dark.

Many plants died without light. Then the plant eaters had no food. When they died out, the meat eaters had no food. Then the dinosaurs became extinct.

Lesson Review

1. What does extinct mean?
2. What are two ideas about why the dinosaurs are extinct?

Think! What do you think happened to the dinosaurs?

THINKING

Skills

Learning to tell cause and effect

Suppose it is a warm and sunny day. If clouds move in front of the sun, you may feel cooler. The moving of the clouds is the cause. A cause makes something happen. Feeling cooler is the effect. An effect is what happens.

Practice

1. Put some water into a jar. Try to read words through the water.
2. Put some dirt into the jar with the water. See if you can read through the water now.
3. Adding dirt is the cause. What is the effect?

Apply

A plant that is grown in a box may not be healthy. What cause can you find for the plant not being healthy?

3. How can we learn about dinosaurs?

Getting Started Flatten a ball of clay. Press your thumb into it. Now take your thumb out. What happened?

Words to Know
fossils
skeleton

No one has ever seen a live dinosaur. But people have found clues about them. Some have found teeth, bones, and footprints. Others have found nests with dinosaur eggs. You read about dinosaur eggs on page 82.

▲ Fossil digging

▲ Dinosaur egg fossils

The eggs and nests have turned into rock. The footprints also have turned into rock. All these clues are called **fossils**.

Most fossils are found in rocks. Scientists study fossils. They want to know about living things of long ago. They also want to know what the earth was like long ago.

▲ Dinosaur footprint fossil

Some fossils are bones. All the bones of an animal make up a **skeleton**. Scientists may find only a few bones. Then they use these clues to tell what the dinosaur looked like. Look at the bone the boy is touching. What part of the skeleton do you think this bone belongs to?

Once, a scientist found a dinosaur skeleton. It did not have a head. Later, he found a head that he thought might belong to the skeleton. He put this head on the skeleton. For many years, people came to see it.

Find out what poets have to say about dinosaurs. Read the poems, starting on page 110.

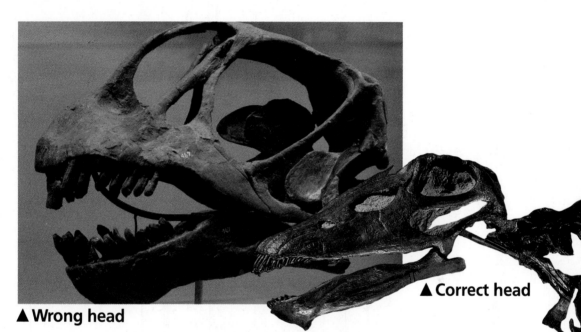

▲ Wrong head

▲ Correct head

Today, scientists know the dinosaur had a different head. They know the first scientist made a mistake.

Lesson Review

1. What are two kinds of fossils?

2. Why do scientists study fossils?

Think! What can people learn from dinosaur footprint fossils?

Can fossils be saved from the trash heap?

There are fossils in the ground in many places. Scientists dig up fossils and study them. The scientists learn a lot from these clues to the past.

But sometimes people build roads over fossils. They also put up homes where fossils are buried. They dump trash on top of fossils.

STS

In one town, people wanted to put trash where some fossils were. But scientists made a plan to save the fossils.

A big hole was dug before the trash was dumped. The scientists took the dirt and rocks from the hole. Then they searched the dirt and rocks for fossils. They made sure that the fossils were saved.

Thinking about it

1. What do you think of the scientists' plan? Is it a good plan? Why or why not?

2. How would you save fossils from being buried by trash?

Using what you learned

Suppose you live in a town that has no playground. Some people want to build one. The new playground would cover up fossils. Would you vote to save the fossils or build the playground? Explain your vote. Take a vote in your class.

4. How do living things become extinct?

Words to Know
pollute
endangered

Getting Started Do you always put trash in the trash can? What would happen if everyone threw their trash on the ground?

The earth is still changing. There are many people. Some are not careful. They pollute the water, land, and air. **Pollute** means they make the water, land, and air dirty. How do people pollute the water, land, and air?

▼ Water pollution

▲ Ring-tailed lemurs

▲ Point Reyes meadowfoam

These living things are **endangered**. There are not many of them left. They may become extinct.

Why do living things become endangered? There are many reasons. Some living things die when people pollute the water, land, and air. Others lose their homes when people build.

▲ California condor

▼ Giant panda

Whooping cranes are endangered. Many of their homes have been destroyed. Scientists studied these birds. They found that most whooping cranes lay two eggs. But sometimes only one chick lives. The first chick that hatches flops around. Sometimes it breaks the other egg. Other times it may hurt the other chick.

▲ Whooping crane eggs

▲ Whooping crane chick

▲ Workers moving a whooping crane egg

People are trying to save the whooping cranes. They take one egg. They put it in the nest of a sandhill crane.

Sandhill cranes care for the egg. They feed the chick that hatches. The chick grows up and joins the rest of the sandhill cranes. How will this help the whooping cranes?

▲ Whooping crane with sandhill cranes

Lesson Review

1. What does pollute mean?
2. What is one reason that animals may become endangered?

Think! How can people help save endangered plants and animals?

Problem Solving

Don't Crack Up!

Whooping cranes are endangered. Suppose you are helping to save the whooping cranes. You must move some whooping crane eggs to sandhill crane nests. Look at an egg. Pretend it is from a whooping crane.

Invent something to carry the egg in safely.

What did you use to make your egg holder? What problems did you have? How does your holder keep the egg safe?

Chapter Connections

Draw the shapes of the word map on a paper.
Fill in the shapes with pictures that show what
the words say.

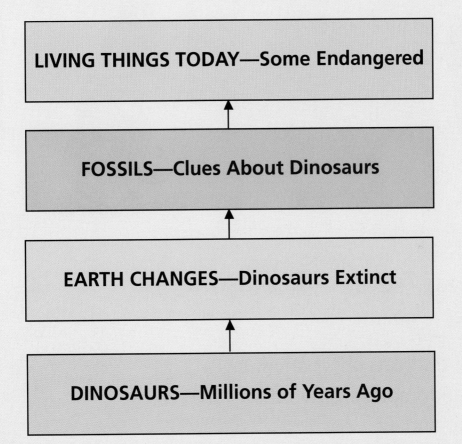

LIVING THINGS TODAY—Some Endangered

FOSSILS—Clues About Dinosaurs

EARTH CHANGES—Dinosaurs Extinct

DINOSAURS—Millions of Years Ago

Writing About Science • Create

How would life be different today if dinosaurs
still lived on the earth? Draw a picture and
write a sentence about it.

Science Words

A. Match each word with a picture.

dinosaur   fossil   skeleton

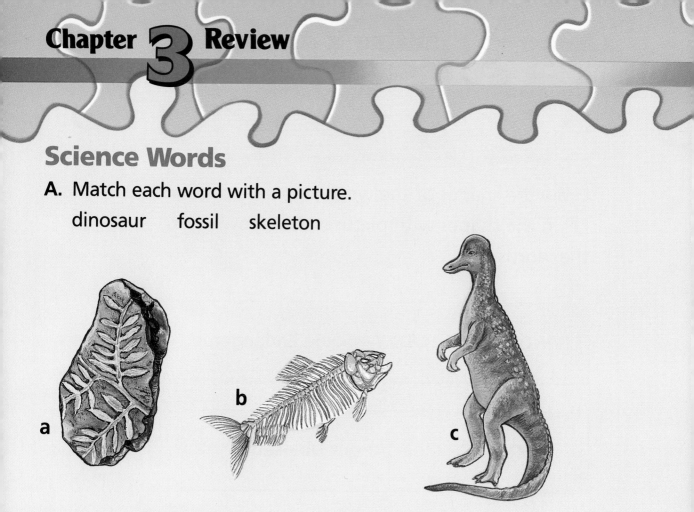

a

b

c

B. Fill in each missing word.

endangered   extinct   meat eater
plant eater   pollute

1. An animal that eats other animals is a _____.

2. Garbage and smoke are two things that can _____ water and air.

3. You can never see a live dinosaur because dinosaurs are _____.

4. An animal that eats only plants is a _____.

5. When there are not many of one kind of animal left on earth, that animal is _____.

Science Ideas

1. Which animal is not a dinosaur?
   Tell how you know.

2. What is one idea about how the dinosaurs became extinct?
3. Give three examples of fossils.
4. How do living things become endangered?

Applying Science Ideas

People build roads and houses. How can building be a problem to scientists who study fossils?

Using Science Skills

There is a storm at night. When you wake up in the morning, many tree branches have fallen to the ground. What could be the cause of this?

Careers

Fossil Scientist

David Gillette is a **fossil scientist.** He digs up and studies fossils. Fossils are clues about what life was like long ago.

David studied hard in school. While he was in school, he also had a job digging fossils. "I loved it," David says. Now he digs up fossils for the state of Utah. He also travels around the world. He has found dinosaur bones in India. David helped dig up the world's longest dinosaur in New Mexico. "I like to study dinosaurs," he says. "They tell us a lot about the past."

Connecting Science Ideas

1. What if you were a scientist like David Gillette. What kinds of dinosaur fossils would you like to find? Tell why.   **Careers; Chapter 3**

2. How is the seed of a plant like the egg of a bird?   **Chapter 1; Chapter 2**

3. Some wildflowers in our country are endangered. Make a list of some reasons why.
   Chapter 2; Chapter 3

4. You learned about two ways animals are grouped. What are some ways to group the plants you saw in Chapter 2?   **Chapter 1; Chapter 2**

5. You read that dinosaurs had no feathers or fur. What kind of body covering might they have had?   **Chapter 1; Chapter 3**

Calculator Connection

How many seeds are in 10 apples? Make a guess. Let your classmates help you eat the apples. Count the number of seeds in all of the apples. Use a calculator to find the total number of seeds. Was your guess close?

**Poems
from**

DINOSAURS

Selected by

LEE BENNETT HOPKINS

Illustrated by Murray Tinkelman

Dinosaurs are no longer alive, but they will come to life as you read these poems.

Dinosaurs

Dinosaurs
Do not count,
Because
They are all
Dead:

None of us
Saw them, dogs
Do not even
Know that
They were there—

But they
Still walk
About heavily
In everybody's
Head.

Valerie Worth

Fossils

Older than
books,
than scrolls,

older
than the first
tales told

or the
first words
spoken

are the stories

in forests that
turned to
stone

in ice walls
that trapped the
mammoth

in the long
bones of
dinosaurs—

the fossil
stories that begin
Once upon a time

Lilian Moore

What if...

What if...
    You opened a book
    About dinosaurs
And one stumbled out
And another and another
    And more and more pour
Until the whole place
Is bumbling and rumbling
And groaning and moaning
    And snoring and roaring
And dinosauring?

What if...
    You tried to push them
    Back inside
But they kept tromping
Off the pages instead?
    Would you close the covers?

Isabel Joshlin Glaser

Reader's Response

Which poem did you like best?

Tell one reason why you liked it so much.

DINOSAURS

📖 Responding to Literature

1. Make up a story about dinosaurs that begins "Once upon a time..." Tell your story to your classmates, then listen to theirs.

2. No one has ever seen a living dinosaur. How do we know so much about them?

3. Pretend you had a dinosaur as a pet. Where would you keep it? What would you feed it? What would you do together?

📖 Books to Enjoy

Patrick's Dinosaurs by Carol Carrick
Patrick sees dinosaurs everywhere! Are they really following him? You will find out if you read the book.

Baby Dinosaurs by Helen Roney Sattler
Have you ever wondered what a newly hatched dinosaur was like? Scientists have found fossils of baby dinosaurs. You can read all about them in this book.

SCIENCE HORIZONS

PHYSICAL SCIENCE

Chapter 4

Learning About Matter

Look at the many things you can make with salt dough. You can make a necklace or a candle holder. You can make a picture, a puppet, or a piggy bank. You can shape, roll, and cut salt dough. You can make almost anything you want.

Salt, flour, and water are mixed together to make dough. The dough is like clay. How is the dough different from the things used to make it?

In this chapter you will learn how things are different from each other. You will find out how they can change. And you will learn to measure things.

1. What is matter?

Words to Know

matter
solid
liquid
gas

Getting Started   Look at these objects. Which objects can fit in a shoebox? Find out!

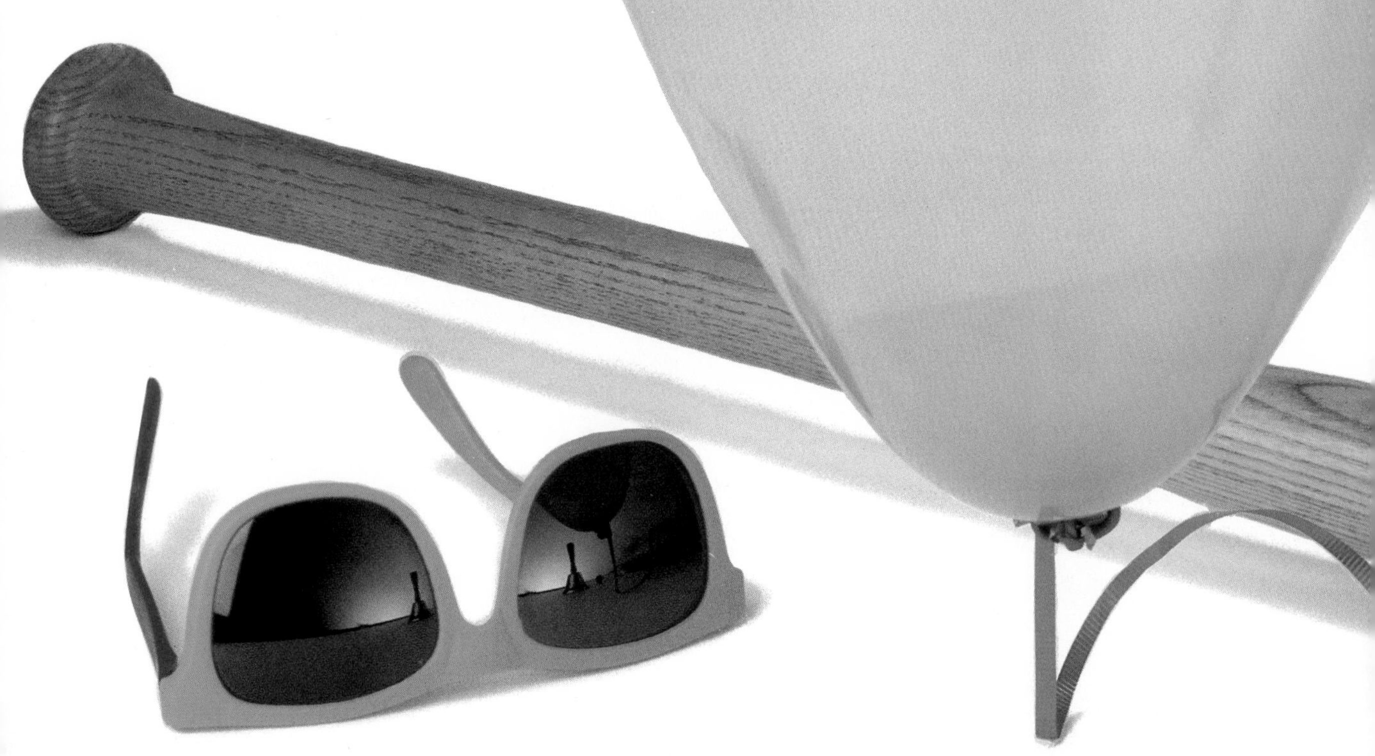

All things are made of **matter**. Things look different. This is because they are made of different kinds of matter. The baseball bat is made of wood. What kinds of matter are the other objects made of?

120

All matter takes up space. Some matter takes up a lot of space. Some matter takes up only a little space. Which of these objects takes up the least space?

Carlos and Maria had a mystery on their hands. See if you can solve it as you read **Ice Pops Aplenty** in Horizons Plus.

One form of matter is a solid. A **solid** has its own shape. If you put a solid in a jar, its shape stays the same. This block did not change shape. What different shapes do these solids have?

▼ Solid matter

▲ Liquid matter

A second form of matter is liquid. A **liquid** does not have a shape of its own. If you put a liquid into a jar, it takes the shape of that jar. Look at the pictures. Why did the shape of the green liquid change?

▲ Gas in balloons

▼ Tank of gas to fill
balloons

A third form of matter is a gas. Like a liquid, a gas does not have its own shape. A **gas** spreads out to fill up whatever it is in. You can see solids and liquids. You cannot see most gases.

Lesson Review

1. What is matter?
2. How are solids, liquids, and gases different from each other?

Think! What solids, liquids, and gases did you use today?

Skills

Making a table

A solid has its own shape. A liquid takes the shape of whatever it is in. A gas fills what it is in. Look at the drawings on this page. They show solids, liquids, and gases.

Solids

Liquids

Gas

air

Practice

1. Copy the table shown.
2. Look at the drawings.
3. Write the names of the solid items under "Solid" in the table. Write the names of the liquids under "Liquid". Write the name of the gas under "Gas".

Solid	Liquid	Gas

Apply

Look around the classroom. Find solids, liquids, and gases. Write the names of the things you find in the table that you made.

2. How can matter change?

Getting Started What happens to an ice cube in the sun? Draw how it changes. Try it and see.

Words to Know
water vapor

Water is one kind of matter. It can have different forms. You can ice-skate on solid water. You can play in liquid water. After you play, your skin dries. As your skin dries, the water changes to a gas. When water is a gas it is called **water vapor**.

You cannot see water vapor. What forms of water are shown in the pictures?

Matter can change from one form to another. Heating can make matter change form. Cooling can also make matter change form.

Carlotta the Great used gas to make her balloon fly. Read how she did it in **The Big Balloon Race,** page 168.

▼ Liquid gold

▼ Solid gold

This gold was a solid. Then it melted and became a liquid. Now it is a solid again. What made the gold change?

Sometimes you can see matter change form. You can see an ice cube melt. You can see solid matter change to a liquid. But you cannot see water in a puddle turn into water vapor. Look at these pictures. What change can you see? What change can you not see?

Lesson Review

1. What are three forms of water?
2. How can a solid be changed to a liquid and then back to a solid?

Think! Why is it useful to change the form of water?

Problem Solving

Cup of Goo

You know that solids have their own shapes. Liquids and gases take the shapes of the objects they are in. Read the card. It tells how to make a kind of matter. Do what the card says. Now test the matter. **Be careful!** Do not eat this matter.

Is this strange matter a solid, a liquid, or a gas?

How can you test your matter? What will happen if you leave your matter overnight? Find out.

Goo Recipe

125 milliliters water in a cup

5 drops green food coloring

2 packs plain gelatin

Mix the water and food coloring. Sprinkle the gelatin on the water. Wait 1 minute. Stir 5 minutes. Chill 1 hour.

3. How can we measure matter?

Getting Started Use your hands to measure your desk. How many hands long is your desk?

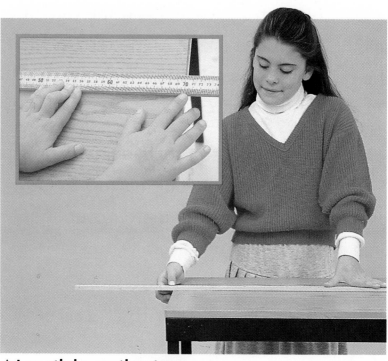

▲ Length in centimeters

You can measure matter. These tools are called metersticks. They measure length. **Length** is how long something is. You can also use these tools to measure how wide or how tall something is. Metersticks measure length in centimeters and meters. How long are the scissors and the desk?

All matter takes up space. The space that matter takes up is called **volume**. These tools measure volume. They can measure the volume of solids that are powders. They can measure the volume of liquids. They measure the volume of these things in milliliters.

▼ Volume in milliliters

This tool is called a **balance**. It shows which object has the most matter. The balance works like a seesaw. The side with more matter goes down. The side with less matter goes up. What happens if two things have the same amount of matter?

▼ Using a balance

Mass is a measure of how much matter there is in an object. Mass is measured in grams. Heavy things have more matter than light things. Heavy things have a greater mass than light things. The balls shown on the balance have the same volume. But one has a greater mass. Which has the most matter?

Lesson Review

1. What is length?
2. What is volume?
3. What is mass?

Think! What tool would you use to find out how much sugar is in a sugar bowl?

ACTIVITY

Explore Together
Which thing has the most matter?

You need

Planner balance • 2 chalkboard erasers • 2 same size shoes • 2 same size building blocks • posterboard

What to do

All **1.** Look at an eraser, a shoe, and a building block. Guess which has the most matter. Guess which has the least matter.

Writer **2.** Make a chart like the one shown.

Helper **3.** Place the three objects on the chart where you think they belong.

	Most Matter	Less Matter	Least Matter
Guess			
Test			

Leader **4.** Use the other three objects and a balance to test the Helper's guesses.

Helper **5.** Put the objects on the chart where they belong.

What did you find out?

All, Writer **1.** How does your guess compare with what you measured?

Reporter **2.** Share your results with the class.

134

Chapter Connections

Write a sentence about something you learned in this chapter. Use the word map to help you.

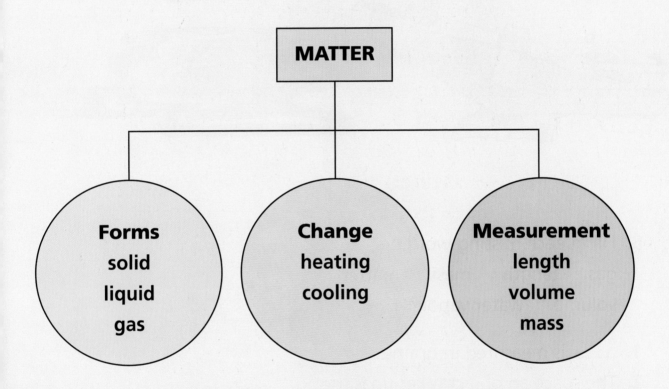

Writing About Science • Classify

Write the word "matter" in the middle of your paper. Around it, write the names of different kinds of matter you know. Put a green circle around liquids. Put a blue circle around solids. Put a red circle around gases.

Science Words

A. Match each word with a picture.

balance   liquid   solid

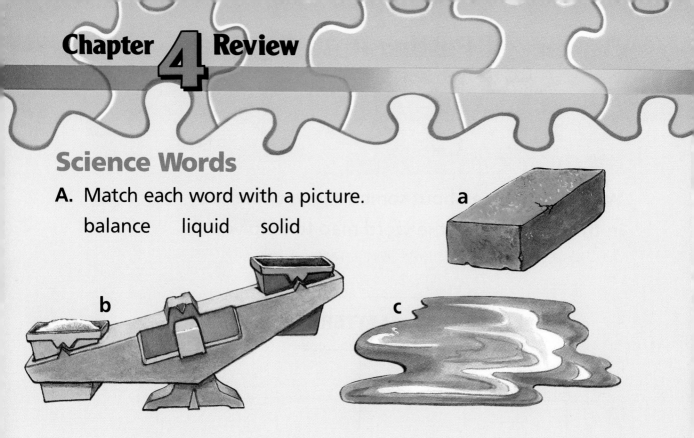

B. Fill in each missing word.

gas   length   mass   matter
volume   water vapor

1. _____ is measured in grams.
2. The space an object takes up is the _____ of the object.
3. Most objects in the form of a _____ cannot be seen.
4. When you measure how long something is, you find out its _____.
5. All objects are made of _____.
6. Liquid water can change into _____.

Science Ideas

1. Name three forms of matter.

2. Which form of matter has its own shape?

3. Describe one way matter changes form.

Applying Science Ideas

What could you use to measure each of these objects?

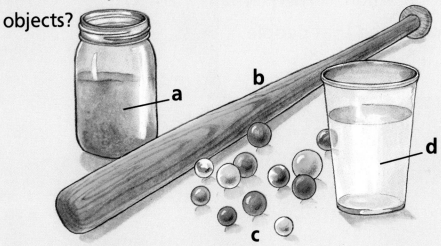

Using Science Skills

Make a chart like the one shown. Add more kinds of matter to your chart. Put checks in the right places.

Kind of matter	Has its own shape	Takes the shape of what it is in	Spreads out to fill what it is in
rock	✔		

Energy in Your Life

It started out like any hot night in New York City. Everyone was trying to cool off. People had their fans set on "High." Then something happened that people still talk about.

All at once the city was dark. The lights were out. The food in freezers melted. Some people were trapped in elevators. Others could not get out of trains in the subway. Why had the whole city come to a stop? There was no electrical energy!

In this chapter you will learn about four kinds of energy. You will see how each one is important to you.

1. What are some forms of energy?

Words to Know

energy
light
heat
sound
electricity

Getting Started Which senses do you use to learn about light, sound, and heat?

There are many forms of energy. Light, sound, and heat are forms of energy. You can see, hear, or feel these forms of energy.

Energy is needed to change things. Energy is needed to make things move. The more something is changed or moved, the more energy is needed.

Light is the form of energy that you can see. Some objects give off their own light. The sun and the stars give off light. Look at the pictures. What else gives off light?

People use light in many ways. At home you use a lamp to read. On a camping trip you may use a flashlight to find something. Think of other times when you use light. Where does the light come from?

▼ Lightning bug

▼ Flashlight

▼ Lightning bolt

Heat is another form of energy. **Heat** energy is used to change matter. How is heat changing the objects in these pictures?

People use heat in many ways. When it is cold outside, heat is used to warm homes. People heat water so they can take baths and wash dishes. Families use heat to cook food and dry clothes. Many workers use heat on their jobs.

These people are using another form of energy. **Sound** is a form of energy you can hear. Look at the pictures. What sounds are being made? How do sounds help keep us safe?

Sounds can tell you many things. Find out some of them in **The House That Groaned** in Horizons Plus.

▲ Electricity used for light

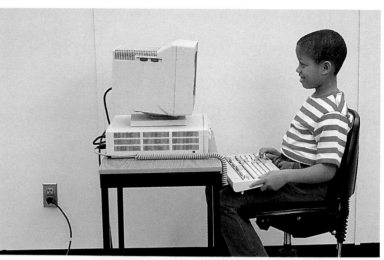

▲ Machine using electricity

Electricity is a form of energy used for light and heat, and to run machines. Name some things in your home that use this form of energy. Sometimes the electricity stops. What is your home like when this happens? On pages 138 and 139 you read about what a city was like without electricity.

Some things that use electricity do not plug into a wall outlet. Where does this truck get its electricity?

Energy can be changed from one form to another. A toaster uses electricity. In a toaster, electricity is changed to heat. The heat toasts the bread.

Often one form of energy is changed into two or more forms. A television uses electricity. It changes electricity into light and sound.

▲ Electricity changes to light and sound.

▲ Electricity changes to heat.

Lesson Review

1. What are four forms of energy?
2. How can each form of energy be used?
3. Name an object that changes one form of energy into another form.

Think! How is energy used in your school?

Is a solar car the best way to go?

Most cars run on gas. But someday there may be no gas left. So a new kind of car is being made. It does not need gas. It runs on energy from the sun.

The solar car has tiny boxes on its roof. They are called solar cells. On a sunny day they turn light into electricity. Some of this electricity makes the car run. The rest of it goes into a battery. The car can run for about an hour, using only the battery.

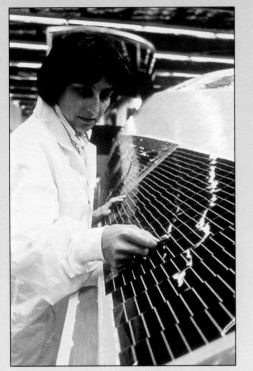

Now there are only a few solar cars. They are small, and they are slow. On cloudy days they cannot go very far.

But someday many people may want to drive solar cars. They do not cost much to use. The cost is low because the sun's light is free. They do not use up gas, and they do not make the air dirty.

Thinking about it

1. Why might people buy solar cars?
2. Why would people not buy solar cars?

Using what you learned

Pretend you have a solar car. Make a chart. Draw a box for each daylight hour in a day. Check the sky. If the sun is out for most of an hour, write "S" in that box. If most of an hour is cloudy, write "C." How many hours could you drive your car that day?

2. What does light do?

Getting Started   Suppose you turn on a lamp in a dark room. How quickly does the room fill with light?

Light moves in straight lines. Nothing moves faster than light. But it still takes time for light to move from place to place.

Light from the sun takes about eight minutes to reach the earth. That may seem like a long time to you. But remember, the sun is very far away.

▲ **Light reflected by water**

Light reflected ▼ by a mirror

Light may be reflected by some things. **Reflected** means that the light hits something and then bounces off.

Some things reflect light better than others do. A mirror reflects almost all the light that hits it. What other things reflect light as a mirror does?

When light strikes some things, it may be absorbed. Light that is **absorbed** is not reflected. The things trap the light.

Some colors absorb more light than other colors do. Dark colors absorb more light than light colors do. That is why at night it is harder to see dark colors than light colors. Less light bounces back from dark colors to your eyes. Which person in the picture is easier to see?

Light can pass through some things. You can see what is behind clear glass. That is because light passes through clear glass.

Some light can pass through wax paper. But wax paper is not like glass. You cannot see clearly through wax paper.

No light passes through a piece of wood. Wood reflects some light. It absorbs the rest of the light. You cannot see through wood.

▲ **Light and dark shadows**

A dark shape formed when an object blocks light is called a shadow. If no light passes through an object, its shadow will be dark. If some light gets through, its shadow will be lighter.

Look at the picture. Why is one shadow lighter than the other?

Lesson Review

1. How does light travel?
2. What happens when light is reflected?
3. What happens when light is absorbed?
4. Why can you see through some things but not others?

Think! How can a shadow show where light is coming from?

Explore Together

What things can light pass through?

You need

Planner — 3 kinds of paper • 4 objects • flashlight

What to do

All — 1. Guess which things light can pass through.

Writer — 2. Copy the chart shown.

Helper — 3. Guess which of the two groups the papers and objects belong to.

Writer — 4. Write down each guess in your chart.

Leader — 5. Shine the flashlight on each paper and object to test your guesses.

Writer — 6. Write what you find out in the chart.

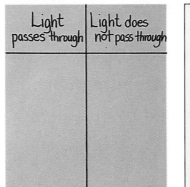

Light passes through	Light does not pass through

What did you find out?

All, Writer — 1. Tell about the things in each group.

2. How are the things in a group alike?

Reporter — 3. Share what you find out with the class.

3. What does heat do?

Words to Know
fuels
friction

Getting Started Do you like eggs fried or hard boiled? How does heat change an egg?

Heat comes from sunlight. Heat also comes from burning things. Things that are burned to give heat are called **fuels**. Oil, gas, wood, and coal are kinds of fuels.

Heat also comes from friction. There is **friction** when two things are rubbed together. Rub your hands together fast. You can feel the heat.

Heat always moves from a warmer place to a cooler place. You cannot see heat move, but you can feel it.

Heat moves through some kinds of matter more quickly than through other kinds. Most pans are made of metal. Heat moves quickly through metal. That is why the food gets hot. Why do you think the handles of some pans are made from wood?

▲ How heat moves

Sometimes people want to slow down the movement of heat. They use things that do not let heat move quickly. Look at the wooden paddle in the picture. The wood keeps heat from moving quickly through the paddle. A heavy coat keeps heat from moving quickly away from your body.

Lesson Review

1. Where does heat energy come from?
2. How does heat always move?
3. Through what kind of matter does heat move quickly?

Think! In what ways do people use things that slow the movement of heat?

THINKING

Skills
Telling what may happen

You know that heat moves quickly through some things. It moves slowly through others. A coat will slow down heat. You can guess that you will stay warmer with a coat on.

Practice

1. On a warm day you do not need to worry about losing heat. On a cold day you want to keep heat in your body.

2. Think about how the weather changed from June to January. What may happen to the number of people wearing coats?

Apply

Suppose that it is a cold day. A student is making the choice of wearing a coat or a sweater. What do you think the student will choose? Tell why.

Words to Know
vibrate

Getting Started Be as quiet as you can. Do you still hear sounds? What do you hear?

▲ Cymbal vibrating

▲ Vibrating strings

Sound energy comes from things that vibrate. Objects **vibrate** when they move back and forth. Most things vibrate too fast for you to see. Tap your pencil on your desk. Your pencil makes a sound. But you cannot see it vibrate. What is vibrating in each picture?

Sound energy moves away from the object that vibrates. The sound moves away in all directions. Think about tossing a rock into water. Circles move away from where the rock went in. This is something like the way sound moves.

▲ **Rock hitting water**

Sound energy moves through all kinds of matter. When you shout, sound moves through the air. When you hit a nail, sound moves through the metal and the air. Whales call to each other under the water. The sounds they make move through the water.

▼ **Whales under water**

Have you ever *seen* music? Make your own music when you try **MUSICSHAPES**.

Sound energy can make things move. The boy hits a gong. The gong vibrates and makes the air move. The sounds you hear can be loud or soft. Hit the gong hard and a loud sound is made. What happens if the gong is hit softly?

Sometimes loud sounds hurt your ears. These people work near loud sounds. How do they keep loud sounds from hurting their ears?

Some objects absorb sound energy. This means that they trap the sound. Soft things absorb much sound. How can a carpet make a room a quiet place?

Lesson Review

1. What causes sound energy?
2. How does sound energy move?
3. What kinds of things absorb sound?

Think! What objects in your classroom do not absorb much sound energy?

Problem Solving
Sounds Good to Me!

Kazoos make sounds. You can make a simple kazoo. Get a cardboard tube. Make a hole in it as shown. Place a piece of paper on one end. Hold the paper in place with a rubber band. Hum into the open end.

What makes the best kazoo?

Try many kinds of paper. Try foil, too. What kind of paper makes the best kazoo? How well does foil work? Find out.

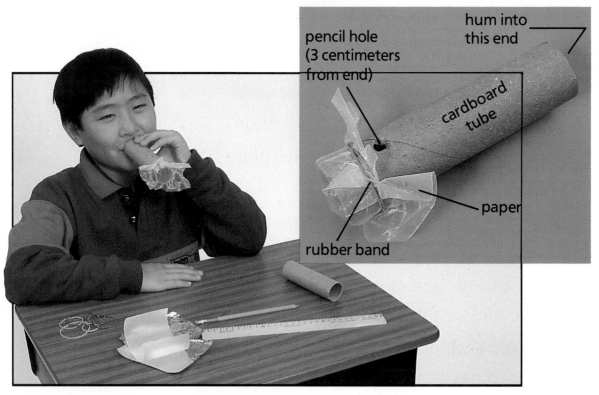

pencil hole (3 centimeters from end)

hum into this end

cardboard tube

paper

rubber band

Chapter Connections

Draw pictures that tell about the kinds of energy shown on the word map. Write a sentence about each picture.

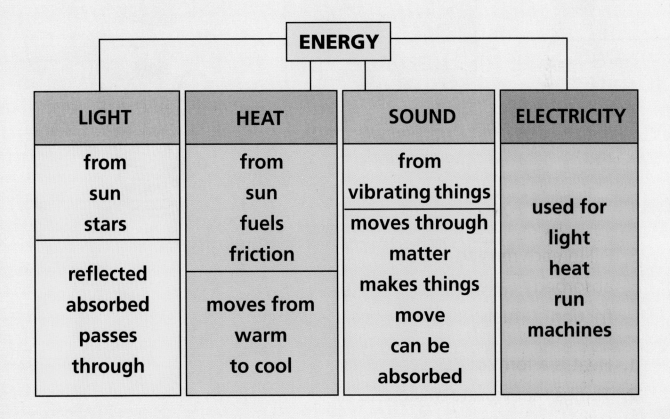

LIGHT	HEAT	SOUND	ELECTRICITY
from sun stars	from sun fuels friction	from vibrating things	used for light heat run machines
reflected absorbed passes through	moves from warm to cool	moves through matter makes things move can be absorbed	

The diagram branches from **ENERGY** at the top.

Writing About Science • Describe

Think about all the sounds you hear in school.
Write a sentence about one of these sounds.

Chapter 5 Review

Science Words

A. Match each word with a picture.

heat   light   reflected   vibrate

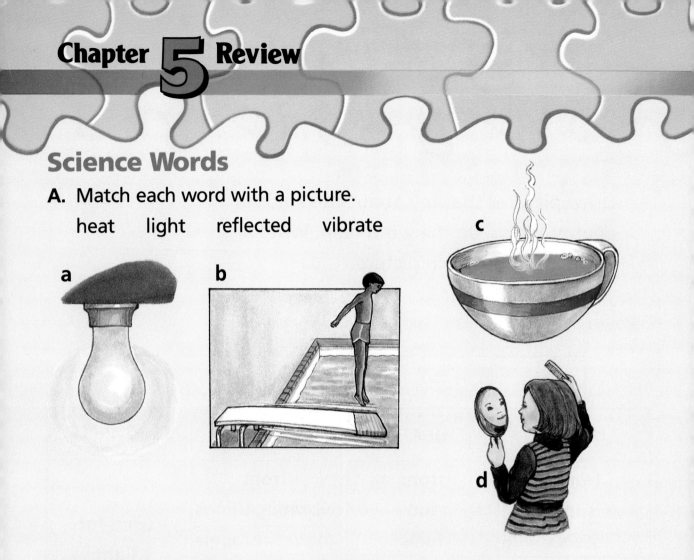

B. Fill in each missing word.

absorbed   electricity   energy
friction   fuels   sound

1. Heat is a form of _____.
2. Things that vibrate make _____.
3. When sound is trapped it is _____.
4. Many machines run on _____.
5. Oil and gas are kinds of _____.
6. Heat made when two things are
   rubbed together comes from _____.

Science Ideas

1. Which picture shows light energy?

2. A radio changes electricity into what other form of energy?

3. Why can you see yourself in a mirror?

4. Why will a tree form a darker shadow than clear glass?

5. What causes friction?

6. Will heat move more quickly through metal or wood?

7. How is sound energy produced?

8. Will metal or cloth absorb more sound?

Applying Science Ideas

In what ways are solar cars better than cars that run on gas?

Using Science Skills

Think about two pots of hot soup. The cover is left off one pot. In which pot will the soup stay warmer? Explain your answer.

Careers

Electrician

"I was always interested in electricity," says Dmitri Lisquez. "I built some radios when I was young." Now Dmitri is an **electrician.** He works for the state of Michigan. Dmitri checks wires in buildings. He makes sure the wires are safe.

Dmitri had to learn a lot to do his job. He went to high school. Next he had many years of training. Then Dmitri took tests for his job. Dmitri likes his job very much. "It is important to keep houses safe for people," Dmitri says.

Connecting Science Ideas

1. Suppose Dmitri came to inspect your home. Make a list of all the things that use electricity to show him.   **Careers; Chapter 5**

2. When does matter change form? When does energy change form?   **Chapter 4; Chapter 5**

3. You read about when the lights went out in New York City. Freezers went off. What happened to the ice in the freezers? Why did this happen?   **Chapter 4; Chapter 5**

4. Where does heat come from? What can heat do?   **Chapter 4; Chapter 5**

5. What forms of matter can sound move through? What forms of matter can light move through?   **Chapter 4; Chapter 5**

Unit Project

Make a musical sound maker. Try using boxes, rubber bands, straws, or bottles. Try to make different sounds. Write how you can change the sounds. Let others try to make music with your sound maker.

from

THE BIG BALLOON RACE

by Eleanor Coerr

Pictures by Carolyn Croll

It's the day of the big balloon race.
Ariel's mother, Carlotta the Great,
will race in her balloon Lucky Star.
Ariel wishes she could go along.
Will her wish come true?

BALLOONS, BALLOONS!

It was the day
of the big balloon race.
Ariel got up early
and hurried to her mother's room.
"Please," she asked, "can I go up
in the balloon with you?"
Carlotta the Great
was putting on her blue dress
with the fancy gold braid.
"You are too young," she said,
"and winning a race
is hard work."
"But I can help," said Ariel.
Carlotta smiled.
"You can help by riding
in the buggy with your father
to the finish line."
"Oh, thumps!" said Ariel.
Sadly, she went outside.

Balloon Farm was a strange farm.
In the yard
half-filled balloons sat
like giant mushrooms.
People came from all over
to buy balloons
made by Mr. Myers.
Ariel watched her father
fold Carlotta's balloon, *Lucky Star*.
"I wish I could be an aeronaut
like Mama," she said.
"When you are older,"
said Mr. Myers.
"Now it is time to go."
Carlotta, Ariel, and Mr. Myers
climbed into the buggy.
Lucky Star followed in a wagon.

There was a great whoop-de-doo
at the fairgrounds.
Thousands of people were there
to see the balloon race.
It was a big event in 1882.
OOMPAH! OOMPAH! OOMPAH!
played the band.
Two balloons were already
in the air.

They were tied to the ground
by long ropes.
Acrobats swung from one basket
to the other.
Lucky Star and its net
were spread out on the ground.
PFFFTTTTTT!
Lighter-than-air hydrogen gas
hissed into the balloon.
It slowly grew
until it was taller
than the house
on Balloon Farm.

Twelve strong men
held *Lucky Star* down.
Nearby, another balloon
grew fat and tall.
It was *Flying Cloud,*
a ball of bright colors.
Its captain, Bernard the Brave,
was the best gentleman aeronaut
in America.
Carlotta the Great
was the best lady aeronaut.
It would be a close race.
"I bet you will win,"
Ariel told her mother.
Carlotta gave her a kiss.
"You can sit in the basket
until it is time to go."
Ariel got inside the basket
and talked to Harry the pigeon.
Harry went on every flight.
Sometimes he took messages
from Carlotta to Balloon Farm.
The mayor began a long speech.
He talked on and on.
So Ariel climbed inside
the Odds and Ends box.

It was quieter there,
and cozy and warm.
Soon she was fast asleep.
Ariel did not hear
the mayor's last words.
"There is a south wind," he said,
"so the finish line will be
the other side
of Devil's Punchbowl Lake."
Ariel did not even hear the drums.
TARUUUUUM!
The aeronauts
stepped into their baskets.
The crowd cheered.
Mr. Myers waved to Carlotta.
"Good luck!"
She waved her nobby sailor hat.
"Hands off!" Carlotta ordered.
The men let go of the ropes.
With a jolt, *Lucky Star* took off.

Reader's Response

The balloon took off and Ariel was still inside.
How do you think she felt when she woke up?

THE BIG BALLOON RACE

📖 Responding to Literature

1. Look back in the story. Name some solids, liquids, and gases talked about in the story.
2. Carlotta the Great named her balloon *Lucky Star.* If you had a balloon, what would you name it? Tell why.
3. Pretend you are riding in a balloon. Draw a picture that shows what you might see below you. Label important places.

📖 Books to Enjoy

The Big Balloon Race by Eleanor Coerr
If you would like to find out who won the race, get a copy of the book from the library.

First Flight by David McPhail
A teddy bear causes a lot of trouble on his first airplane trip. Find out what happens when the bear does not follow the rules.

SCIENCE
HORIZONS

Three

EARTH SCIENCE

The Sun

Have you ever played a game with your shadow? Here is a poem about someone racing his shadow.

SHADOW RACE

Every time I've raced my shadow
When the sun was at my back,
It always ran ahead of me,
Always got the best of me.
But every time I've raced my shadow
When my face was toward the sun,
I won.

Shel Silverstein

In this chapter you will learn to use
the sun to tell time. You will also
learn other things about the sun.

1. What is the sun like?

Getting Started Think about a tiny light bulb being used to light a large room. How is this bulb like the sun?

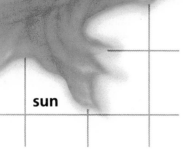

sun

When you look at the sky at night, you see many stars. A **star** is an object in the sky that gives off light. The sun is a star. The **sun** is the star closest to the earth.

Like other stars, the sun gives off light. The light comes from glowing gases. The sun is a huge ball of glowing gases.

earth

The sun is much larger than the earth. But the sun looks small because it is so far away. Large things that are far away look small.

Think about how an airplane looks as it flies away. It seems to get smaller and smaller. Many stars you see at night are much bigger than the sun. Why do they look smaller than the sun?

▲ Sunlight hitting the earth

Light from the sun hits the earth. It hits both the land and the water. Some of the light that hits the earth is changed to heat. The heat warms the earth. Then the warm earth heats the air around it.

Lesson Review

1. How is the sun like the stars you see at night?
2. Why do the sun and the stars look small?

Think! Why is the sun important to living things on the earth?

Skills

Looking at flat and solid shapes

What shape is a real orange? An orange is round, like a ball. What shape is an orange in a picture? In a picture, an orange looks like a flat circle. A flat circle is like an orange. Both are round.

Practice

1. Look at the cube and its shadow. The shadow is a flat square.

2. Look at a real ball. Draw the shadow you think the ball will make. Now hold the ball in the sunlight. What kind of shadow does it make?

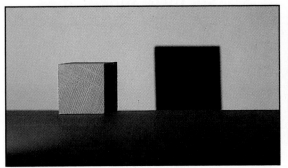

 ▲ Cube

 ▲ Ball

Apply

Look at the box. Draw the shadows you think the box will make. Hold the box in the sunlight. What flat shapes match the solid box shape?

2. Why does the sun seem to move?

Getting Started   Stand up. Slowly turn around in place. Notice how the things around you seem to move.

When you spin, you move around in place. The things around you do not move. But they seem to move around you as you spin.

The sun seems to move across the sky every day. Every morning the sun rises in the east. Every evening the sun sets in the west. But the sun does not move.

The sun rises and sets because the earth rotates. **Rotate** means to spin. A globe can be used to show how the earth rotates. A globe is a model of the earth. It is round like the earth, and it can rotate like the earth. In what other ways is a globe like the earth?

▲ Rotating a globe

Look at the picture. Half the globe is in the light. Half the globe is in the dark. This is like day and night on the earth.

▼ Day

▲ Night

The earth rotates once in about 24 hours. The sun seems to move across the sky because the earth rotates. We have day and night because the earth rotates.

As the earth rotates, half of it faces the sun. It is day on this half. The other half of the earth faces away from the sun. It is night on that half.

Lesson Review

1. Why does the sun seem to move across the sky?
2. Explain why the earth has day and night.

Think! Suppose the earth rotated once every 10 hours. How long would a day be?

184

Explore Together

What causes day and night?

ACTIVITY

You need

Planner globe • clay • toothpick • flashlight • meterstick

What to do

Leader **1.** Look at a globe. Find where you live. Mark the spot with clay and a toothpick.

Helper **2.** Place the globe about 2 meters in front of a flashlight.

Leader **3.** Turn the globe so that the toothpick is in light.

Writer **4.** Draw a picture to show that it is daytime where you live.

Helper **5.** Guess what will happen if you rotate the globe one half turn.

Leader **6.** Rotate the globe one half turn.

Writer **7.** Draw a picture to show that it is now night where you live.

What did you find out?

All, Writer **1.** What caused the toothpick to be in day and then in night?

Reporter **2.** Share your answers with the class.

185

3. How can you tell time by the sun?

Words to Know

shadow

Getting Started Pretend there are no clocks. How would you know when it was morning?

Long ago, people did not have clocks. They told the time of day by looking at where the sun was in the sky.

In the morning, the sun rises in the east. This is called sunrise. When it is noon, the sun is high in the sky. At the end of the day, the sun sets in the west. This is called sunset.

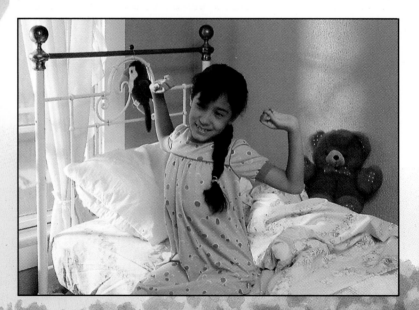

These people did not look at a clock. They are using the sun to tell time. How do they know that it is noon?

Think about where the sun is in the sky right now. What time of day is it? What were you doing at sunrise? What will you be doing at sunset?

You can also tell time by looking at shadows. A **shadow** is a dark shape formed when an object blocks light. You read a poem about shadows on page 177.

You can see how shadows change. Look at the flashlight that is over the top end of the pencil. The shadow of the pencil is short. Now look at the flashlight that is low on one side of the pencil. How does the shadow change?

Do you like riddles? Cassie's aunt does. Test yourself with Cassie as you read **The Riddles of Aunt Red Wing** in Horizons Plus.

Shadows can form when light from the sun hits an object. As the sun seems to move across the sky, a shadow changes. The shadow becomes longer or shorter. It moves from place to place, too. Watching these changes in shadows can help you tell the time of day.

Lesson Review

1. Tell where in the sky the sun is at sunrise, noon, and sunset.
2. How do shadows help people tell time?

Think! What problems might people have using only the sun to help them tell time?

ACTIVITY

Problem Solving
Time to Get Up!

It is Wednesday evening. You are planning to go on a hike with a friend and her family. You are leaving on Saturday morning. Your friend said to get up at sunrise. The sun does not rise at the same time each day.

How can you find out the time sunrise will be on Saturday?

Think about ways to find out. What time did the sun rise on Thursday and Friday? What time will the sun rise on Saturday?

Chapter Connections

Copy the word map on your paper. Leave out some of the important words. Trade papers with a classmate. Fill in the missing words.

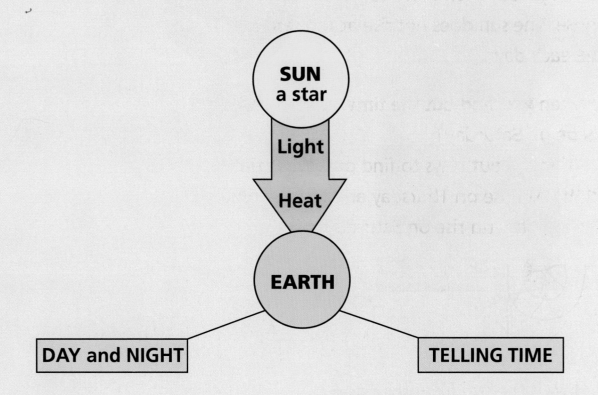

SUN
a star

Light

Heat

EARTH

DAY and NIGHT

TELLING TIME

Writing About Science • Inform

Read a book about the sun. Then make a sun booklet with five pages. Write a sentence about the sun on each page. Draw a picture to go with each sentence.

Science Words

Match each word with a picture.

rotate   shadow   stars   sun

a

b

c

d

Science Ideas

1. How is the sun like other stars?
2. Why do the stars in the night sky look so small?
3. Why does the sun seem to move across the sky?
4. How could you show how the earth has night and day?

5. Why does the earth have night and day?

6. Which picture shows the sun early in the morning?

7. Where is the sun at noon?

8. Where is the sun late in the evening?

9. How do shadows change as the sun seems to move?

Applying Science Ideas

On your way to school, look at the shadow that a flagpole makes. How will the shadow change by the time you eat lunch? How will the shadow change by the time you leave school?

Using Science Skills

Think about the sun. What flat shape matches the shape of the sun?

Chapter 7

Air and Water

Have you ever heard of a glacier? A glacier is a large body of ice that moves. It forms in places that are very cold. In these places snow falls each year. But not all of it melts. New snow piles on top of snow from years ago. After many years the snow is deep. The snow at the bottom changes to ice.

Sometimes blocks of ice break off from a glacier and fall into the ocean. These blocks are called icebergs. Icebergs float in the ocean.

In this chapter you will learn more about water on the earth. You will also find out why air and water are important to living things.

1. Where is air found?

Getting Started   Fan your hand in front of your face. What do you feel?

Air is a mix of many gases. You cannot see air. But you can feel moving air. You felt moving air when you waved your hand. What is moving the sailboards in the picture?

One of the gases in air is called **oxygen**. Plants and animals must have oxygen to live. People need oxygen too.

Some plants and animals live in water. Living things in water need air. There is air in water. Water plants and animals use this air to live.

You can see that there is air in water. Look at the water in the glass. The water was left for a day. You can see bubbles in the water. The bubbles have air in them. The air bubbles came from the water.

▲ Air bubbles in water

There are many kinds of living things in soil. Plants live in soil. Worms and other animals live in soil too.

▼ Living things in soil

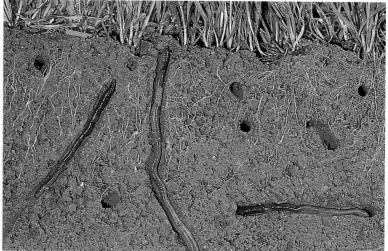

There is air in soil. Look at the picture. Spaces in the soil have air in them. Plants and animals that live in soil use this air.

Lesson Review

What was wrong with Tom's two fish? Find out in **What's the Matter with Melvin and Moofer?** in Horizons Plus.

1. How do you know air is all around you?
2. Name a gas in air that plants and animals need.
3. How can you tell that air is in water and soil?

Think! Whales cannot breathe the air that is in water. Where do they get their air?

Explore

What things have air inside?

Suppose you blow air through a straw into water. You will see air bubbles rise in the water. Other things have air in them. When put in water, these things will also bubble.

ACTIVITY

You need

jar • water • 3 different small objects • 2 white cards

What to do

1. Half fill a jar with water.
2. Place one object into the water. Watch what happens. Decide if the object has air in it.
3. Test two more objects.
4. Label a card "Things With Air." Label another card "Things Without Air." Put each object into one of the groups.

What did you find out?

1. What happened when each object was put in water?
2. Which objects have air in them?

2. Where is water found?

Getting Started Suppose you breathe on a mirror. What might you see?

▼ Breathing on a mirror

Water is found all over the earth. There is water in the air that you breathe. You can see the water when you breathe on a mirror.

Some water in the air is a gas. This gas is called **water vapor**. You cannot see water vapor. But you can see liquid water in the air. Some clouds are made of tiny drops of liquid water. Some are made of tiny pieces of ice.

There are two kinds of water on the earth. Salt water is one kind. The water that fills the oceans is salt water.

▼ Salt water

▼ Fresh water

▲ Puddle

The other kind of water is fresh water. There is fresh water in rivers, ponds, streams, and lakes. What kind of water do you think is in the puddle? What kind of water do you drink?

▲ Icebergs

Some water on the earth is solid. Solid water is called ice. Snow is tiny pieces of ice.

In some places the air is cold all year. Ice and snow do not melt. The North Pole and South Pole are places like this. There are glaciers and icebergs at the poles. You read about glaciers and icebergs on pages 194 and 195.

Lesson Review

1. Where is fresh water found?
2. Where is salt water found?
3. Where are icebergs and glaciers found?

Think! You cannot see water vapor in the air, but you can see clouds. Explain why.

Explore Together

How does water get into the air?

You need

Planner   water • large jar • rubber band • plastic wrap

What to do

Leader   **1.** Half fill a jar with water.

Helper   **2.** Use a rubber band to put plastic wrap over the jar.

Leader   **3.** Put the jar in sunlight.

All   **4.** Look at the jar after a few hours.

Writer   **5.** Write down what you see.

What did you find out?

All, Writer   **1.** What collects on the plastic wrap?

2. How did it get there?

Reporter   **3.** Share what you found out with the class.

Can people live under water?

Some scientists work under the sea. They stay in a lab called *Aquarius.* It is 15 meters under the water. The lab is as big as a bus. The scientists swim outside the lab. They study the fish and the seafloor. Inside the lab they cook and eat. They sleep there, too.

A boat floats on the sea over *Aquarius.* Tubes and wires hook the boat to the lab. They carry air, fresh water, and electricity to people inside the lab.

204

STS

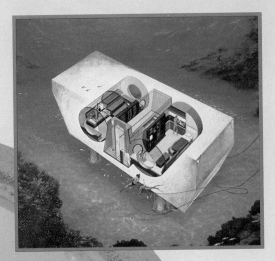

Some people go under the sea for fun. They stay in a hotel on the seafloor, near Florida. A van on land sends air, water, and electricity to the hotel.

Guests swim down to the hotel. Inside they can sleep, eat, and watch movies. Outside they can swim around and watch the fish. They can look at old boats that sank to the seafloor long ago.

Thinking about it

1. Water is all around *Aquarius*. Why do the scientists need to get water from a boat?

2. Some people think living under water will help the sea. Others say it will hurt the sea. Can both ideas be right? How?

Using what you learned

Pretend that you work in a lab under the sea. Tell about one day in your life under water.

3. How are air and water used?

Getting Started What happens if you forget to water a houseplant for many weeks? Why does this happen?

▲ Hot-air balloon

People use air in many ways. Air dries wet clothes hanging on a line. Air is used to fill a beach ball.

People use air to help make things fly. Wind makes a kite fly. The air moving over an airplane wing helps make the plane rise. The cold air outside this balloon makes the balloon rise.

Moving air is wind. Wind energy can be changed into electricity. A windmill does this.

Wind turns the blades of a windmill. The blades turn wheels. The energy in these wheels is changed to electricity. Why can windmills not work all the time?

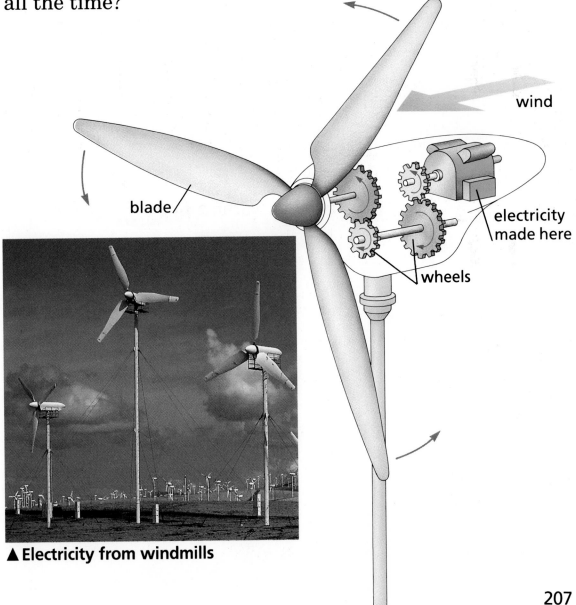

wind

blade

electricity made here

wheels

▲ Electricity from windmills

207

People and other living things need water to stay alive. Your body is made mostly of water. You drink water.

Water is in the foods you eat. Look at the pictures. How does each food look when water is taken out of it?

People use water in many ways. They use water to clean themselves. They use water to wash clothes and dishes. What are some other ways you use water in your home?

▲ Water to keep pets clean

▲ Having fun in water

People also use water for play. Swimming and boating are some ways people have fun with water. How do you have fun with water?

People use water to help carry things from place to place. Big ships carry large loads from place to place. Water makes it easier to move heavy things.

People also use the energy of moving water. They use moving water to make electricity at power plants.

Lesson Review

1. How do people use air?
2. How is moving air used to make electricity?
3. How do people use water?

Think! What are two foods that you must add water to before eating?

THINKING

Skills

Finding out what causes a change

Suppose you have a cup of dry sand. You can tip the cup, and the sand pours out. You can add water to the sand. Wet sand will not pour out as easily. The water causes a change.

Practice

1. Put warm water into a cup.
2. Put a sugar cube in the cup of water. Leave another sugar cube in air.
3. Observe both sugar cubes. One cube will change.
4. Write what causes one sugar cube to change.

Apply

Break a slice of apple. Observe the broken ends. Put one part in water. Leave the other part in air. Tell whether air or water causes an apple to change more.

4. How can air and water be kept clean?

Words to Know
pollute
recycle

Getting Started   Think about the smoke from burning leaves or trash. How does the smoke make air look? What happens if you breathe smoke?

Smoke from cars and trucks makes air dirty. When people make air dirty, they **pollute** it. People also pollute air when they burn leaves or trash.

Polluted air is harmful to living things. It can make people sick. Some people must stay indoors on days when the air is very polluted.

People also pollute water. People dump garbage into water. Things such as food, paper, and cans make water dirty. Oil also pollutes water. What things in the pictures pollute water?

Polluted water makes people sick. It can kill plants and animals that live in water.

▼ Cleaning oil off bird

Bird caught in plastic ▶

213

▲ Putting trash in the right place

People can help keep the air clean. They can use buses or trains instead of cars. They should not burn leaves or trash. How else can people keep air clean?

People can also help keep water clean. They should not dump garbage into water. How else can people keep water clean?

People can help keep the earth clean. These girls are cleaning up trash.

People should throw trash away in the right place. They can also make less trash. One way they can do this is to recycle things. **Recycle** means to use over and over again. People can recycle glass, paper, and cans.

▲ Recycling

Lesson Review

1. How do people pollute air?
2. How do people pollute water?
3. What is one way that people can keep air clean?
4. What is one way people can keep water clean?

Think! How does recycling paper help save trees?

Problem Solving

Make It Crystal Clear

ACTIVITY

Many things can make water dirty. Soil, food, oil, and trash can pollute water. A water filter can help. A filter strains out some of the things in water.

What are the best filters for cleaning dirty water?

Think of how a filter works. Make a plan to find the best way to clean dirty water. Then try your plan.

Chapter Connections

Write two questions about something you learned in this chapter. Use the word map to help you. Trade questions with a classmate. Answer the questions.

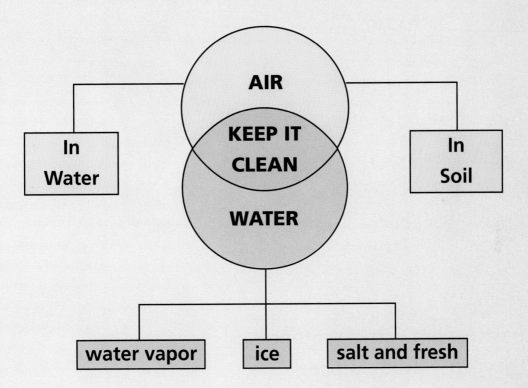

Writing About Science • Persuade

In this chapter you learned that people can recycle things. Make a poster that tells people they should recycle.

Science Words

A. Match each word with a picture.

pollute   recycle

a

b

B. Match each word with a sentence.

air   oxygen   water vapor

1. You cannot see any of the gases that make up _____.

2. Water in the form of a gas is _____.

3. One gas that plants and animals need to live is called _____.

Science Ideas

1. How do you know that air is all around you?

2. How can you tell that air is in water?

3. How are airplanes and hot-air balloons alike?

4. How do you know there is water in the air?

5. What are two kinds of water?

6. How do people use water?

7. How does air become polluted?

8. How does water become polluted?

9. How can air be kept clean?

10. How can water be kept clean?

Applying Science Ideas

Why do some people live under the sea?

Using Science Skills

What caused the change in the flag?

Looking at Weather

Have you ever played with snow? Myron Ace has. Myron lives in Alaska. Alaska is the biggest state in the United States. So Myron wanted his state to have the biggest snowman. Myron and his friends worked hard for 2 weeks. When they were done, they had a huge snowman.

This snowman turned out to be the biggest one in the world! It was over 19 meters tall. But just one day after the snowman was done, the white snow turned brown. A dust storm blew dirt all over it.

In this chapter you will discover what causes weather to change. You will also learn what kinds of clouds make it snow. You will see why it is important to know about the weather.

1. Why do you need to know about the weather?

Words to Know
weather

Getting Started Listen to a weather report. What did you find out?

Weather is what the air outside is like. The air may be warm or cool. It may be wet or dry. The sky may be clear, or it may be cloudy. When you know what the air is like, you know about the weather. What is the weather like now where you live?

If the air changes, the weather changes. It could be warm today and cool tomorrow. What is the air like in the pictures on these pages?

You need to know about the weather every day. You need to know how to dress. If the weather is cold, you will want to wear a coat outside. If it is warm, you will want to wear light clothes. You want to know if you can play outside.

How can you find out about the weather? You cannot see air. Look out a window. How can you tell how warm or how cold the air is?

▲ **Farmers water a dry field**

Many workers need to know about the weather. Farmers need to know if it is going to rain. Truck drivers need to know if the roads will be slippery.

A pilot checks the weather before the plane takes off. The pilot needs to know where any storms are. What other workers need to know about the weather?

Lesson Review

1. What is weather?
2. What kinds of workers need to know about the weather?

Think! What can you do on a sunny day that you cannot do on a rainy day?

Skills

Measuring temperature with a thermometer

You want to go swimming, but the water might be too cool. You can find the temperature of the water by using a thermometer. Look at the thermometer in the drawing. It shows 20 degrees.

Practice

1. Put warm water into one jar. Put cold water into another jar.

2. Put a thermometer into each jar. Watch the thermometers for 2 minutes.

3. Find the temperature of the water in each jar. Read the number next to the top of the red line.

Apply

Stand in a sunny place. Then stand in the shade. Where did you feel warmer? Use a thermometer to find the temperature in each place. Which place has a higher temperature?

2. How hot or cold is the air?

Getting Started   Place a book with a dark cover in a sunny place. Wait 15 minutes. Touch it. What do you notice?

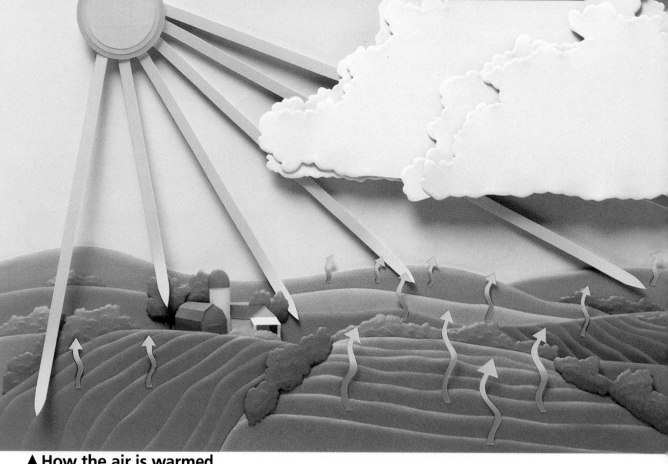

▲ How the air is warmed

The sun warms the earth. Then the earth warms the air around us. The more sunlight there is, the warmer the air is. **Temperature** is how hot or how cold something is.

226

A **thermometer** is a tool that measures temperature. Most thermometers use numbers to show the temperature. A high number means it is warm. A low number means it is cool.

Some thermometers measure the temperature of the air. What are some other ways that thermometers are used?

▲ **Outdoor thermometers**

You must dress the right way in all kinds of weather. Wear warm clothes in cold weather. Do not stay outside too long. How are these children dressed for cold weather?

Wear light clothes in hot weather. Wear a hat in the sun. Drink plenty of water. Your body loses water in hot weather. Play quiet games. What are some good games to play in hot weather?

Lesson Review

1. What is temperature?
2. How is temperature measured?
3. How can you be careful in hot weather?

Think! Why is it usually warmer during the day than at night?

Problem Solving

Hot Spots!

ACTIVITY

Suppose there are people in different rooms of a house. Some people feel warm, others feel cool. It may be that the temperature is not the same in all parts of the house. Temperature may vary within a room too.

Is the temperature the same in all parts of your classroom?

What can you use to help you find out? Where do you think the classroom is the warmest? Where do you think the classroom is the coolest? Find out if you are right.

3. What is wind?

Getting Started Look out the window. How can you tell if the wind is blowing?

▲ Wind vane

Moving air is called wind. You cannot see wind, but you can see that it moves things. We use tools to learn about the wind. A **wind vane** points to where the wind is coming from.

Look at the windsock. The shape of the sock tells you that the wind is blowing hard. In a strong wind it stands out straight. What would a windsock look like when there is no wind?

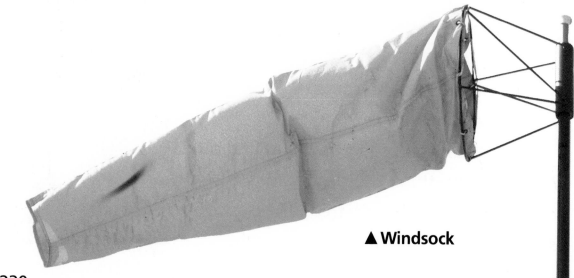

▲ Windsock

230

Gust ▲

▲ Breeze

A **breeze** is a wind that moves gently. You may see leaves flutter when there is a breeze.

On some days, the wind is strong. Kites fly high. People need to hold on to their hats! A short burst of strong wind is called a **gust**.

A **storm** is weather with very strong winds. Often there is much rain or snow. Storm winds can cause high waves along shores.

▲ Storm

A tornado has the strongest winds of all storms. The winds can tear up trees and destroy buildings.

▲ Tornado

Lesson Review

1. What is wind?
2. What does a wind vane do?
3. How is a gust different from a breeze?

Think! Why do airports have windsocks?

Explore

How can you tell the direction of the wind?

Many people need to know wind direction. Hot-air-balloon pilots must know so they can plan trips.

You need

tissue paper • scissors • long pipe cleaner • tape • string

What to do

1. Cut tissue paper as shown. **Be careful!** Scissors can cut you.
2. Lay a pipe cleaner on the top edge of the tissue paper.
3. Fold the paper over the pipe cleaner. Tape the long edge.
4. Make a hoop and tape it as shown. Hang your windsock.

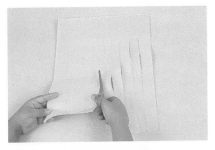

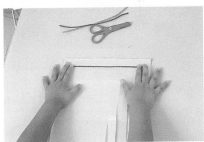

What did you find out?

1. How can you use the windsock to tell wind direction?
2. How can you use the windsock to tell how strong the wind is?

4. What can you learn by watching clouds?

Words to Know
clouds
fog

Getting Started   Wet the chalkboard. Fan it. What happens to the water?

▲ How clouds form

You can learn a lot of things by watching clouds. From them Ruth learned when it was time to ride in a balloon. Read about it in **A Ride in a Pumpkin Balloon** in Horizons Plus.

Clouds are made of tiny drops of water. The water might come from a lake or an ocean. The liquid water changes into a gas called water vapor.

The gas goes into the air. In cool air, the gas changes back to liquid water. In very cold air, the gas changes to bits of ice. The drops of water or bits of ice stay in air as clouds.

Sometimes the tiny drops of water in a cloud join together. They form larger drops. The larger drops cannot stay in the air. So they fall to the earth.

▲ Snow

▲ Rain

▲ Hail

Liquid water that falls from the clouds is rain. If it is very cold, the liquid water freezes. Then sleet may fall. What else may fall from clouds?

▲ Clouds made of ice

There are different kinds of clouds. These clouds are made of tiny bits of ice. Some people think these clouds look like feathers. If you see these clouds, it will probably rain or snow soon.

These white, puffy clouds are seen in fair weather. They look like balls of cotton.

Fair weather clouds ▼

236

These clouds form thick layers. The sky seems to be filled with one big cloud! These thick clouds mean wet weather ahead.

Fog is a cloud that is close to the ground. If you walk through fog, you are inside a cloud. You can feel the tiny drops of water that make the cloud.

▼ Fog

▲ Storm clouds

Read **Storm in the Night,** page 246. It tells about two big storms. One of them happened a long time ago.

When you see dark clouds like these, get ready for a storm. Many storms are not harmful. But some storms can harm living things. A storm with heavy rain can cause floods.

Floods happen when rivers and streams cannot hold all the rainwater. Then the water flows over the land. How are floods a danger to people, plants, and animals?

A blizzard is one kind of winter storm. There is much snow. Strong winds blow the snow around. It is hard to see. The temperature may get very cold. It is dangerous to travel during a blizzard. What do you see in this picture of a blizzard?

▲ Blizzard

Lesson Review

1. What are clouds made of?
2. Draw a cloud you see on a sunny day. Then draw a rain cloud.
3. How can a storm with heavy rain be harmful?

Think! What must happen for rain to turn into sleet?

ACTIVITY

Explore Together

What can you tell by looking at clouds?

You need

Planner thermometer • chart paper • crayons

What to do

Leader 1. Use a thermometer to measure the air temperature outside.

Writer 2. Write the day and temperature on a chart.

Helper 3. On the chart, draw pictures that match the weather.

All 4. Repeat steps **1**, **2**, and **3** for five days.

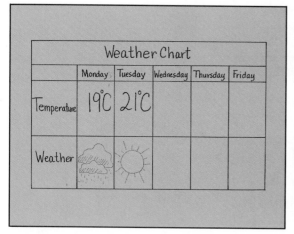

What did you find out?

All, Writer 1. Which clouds are fair-weather clouds?

2. Which clouds are rain clouds?

Reporter 3. Share your results with the class.

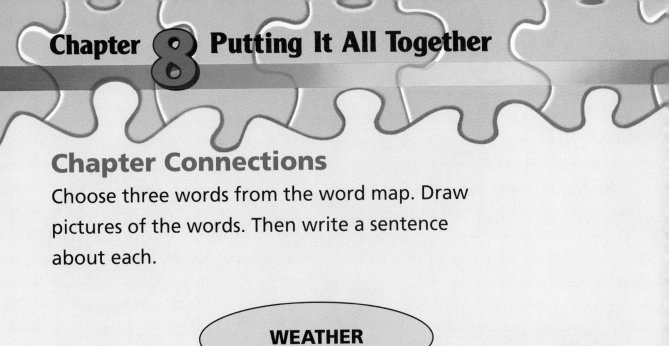

Chapter 8 Putting It All Together

Chapter Connections

Choose three words from the word map. Draw pictures of the words. Then write a sentence about each.

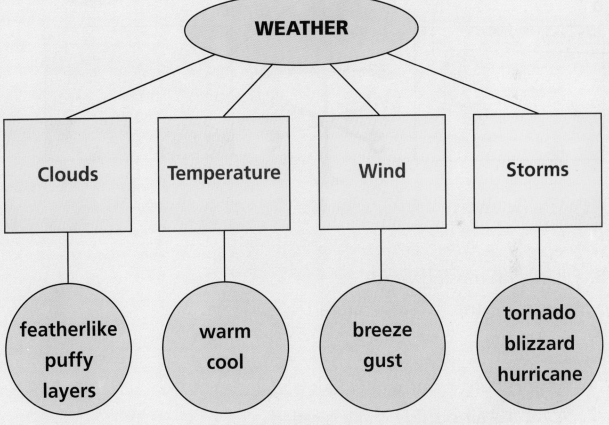

WEATHER

- Clouds
  - featherlike
  - puffy
  - layers
- Temperature
  - warm
  - cool
- Wind
  - breeze
  - gust
- Storms
  - tornado
  - blizzard
  - hurricane

Writing About Science • Narrate

Write a story about a big storm. Share your story with the class.

Science Words

A. Match each word with a picture.

clouds   fog   thermometer   wind vane

a

b

c

d

B. Fill in each missing word.

breeze   gust   temperature

storm   weather

1. A short burst of strong wind is a _____.
2. What the air outside is like is called _____.
3. How hot or cold something is can be called _____.
4. A blizzard is a kind of _____.
5. A gentle wind is a _____.

Science Ideas

1. What kind of weather is this person dressed for?

2. How can you keep safe in very hot weather?

3. What are two kinds of wind?

4. What does a wind vane show you?

5. What weather may these clouds bring?

Applying Science Ideas

This is what you see when you look out the window. Should you go outside or stay in? Explain your choice.

Using Science Skills

Someone moves a thermometer from a freezer to a sunny windowsill. The red line on the thermometer moves up. What does this change tell you?

Careers

Diver

Kathy Griffin grew up near the ocean. When she was growing up, she loved to swim and surf. Now Kathy is a **diver** in Illinois. She teaches at a scuba-diving school.

Kathy's classroom is a big pool. Kathy's students learn to dive safely. They learn to dive in the dark. Then they can dive at night. They learn to take pictures under water, too. When they finish taking lessons, they are ready to dive in rivers, lakes, and oceans. Some students learn to dive for fun. Others need to dive to do their jobs.

Kathy studied diving for two years. Then she had to pass many tests. Now she is a master diver. "I like to help new students," Kathy says. "Diving is hard, but it is fun, too."

Connecting Science Ideas

1. Would you like to learn to dive in a pool, a lake, or the ocean? Tell why.   **Careers; Chapter 7**

2. You read about a lab called Aquarius. Why do people who go there need to know how to dive?   **Chapter 7; Careers**

3. You read how people of long ago told time without clocks. How could clouds stop them from knowing the time?   **Chapter 6; Chapter 8**

4. You read about a very big snowman in Alaska. How could you use that snowman to tell time?   **Chapter 8; Chapter 6**

Calculator Connection

Did you know that 10 centimeters of snow equals 1 centimeter of rain? Use a calculator to help you complete the following table.

Rain (centimeters)	Snow (centimeters)	Rain (centimeters)	Snow (centimeters)
1	10	10	?
3	?	30	?
4	?	?	370

from

Storm in the Night

Written by MARY STOLZ ◆ **Illustrated by PAT CUMMINGS**

Have you ever been afraid of a thunderstorm? Sit on the porch and swing with Thomas and his grandfather. Listen to a good story for a stormy night.

Storm in the night.
Thunder like mountains blowing up.
Lightning licking the navy-blue sky.
And Grandfather? . . . And Thomas? . . . And Ringo, the cat?
They were in the dark.
"We can't read," said Grandfather.
"We can't look at TV," said Thomas.
"Too early to go to bed," said Grandfather.
Thomas sighed. "What will we do?"
"No help for it," said Grandfather, "I shall have to tell you a tale of when I was a boy."
"Let's go out on the porch," said Grandfather.

◆

Grandfather and Thomas sat on the swing, creaking back and forth, back and forth, as thunder boomed and lightning stabbed across the sky.
Ringo's fur rose, and he turned his head from side to side, his eyes wide and wild in the flashes that lit up the night.
"Poor boy," said Thomas. "He's frightened."
"I had a dog when I was a boy," said Grandfather. "He was so scared of storms that I had to hide under the bed with him when one came. He was afraid even to be frightened alone."

"I'm not afraid of thunderstorms, like Ringo and your dog. What was his name?"

"Melvin."

"Is there a story about Melvin?"

"There is. One very good one."

"Tell it," Thomas commanded. "Please, I mean."

"Well," said Grandfather, "when Melvin and I were pups together, I was just as afraid of storms as he was."

"Anyway, the day came when Melvin was out on some errand of his own, and I was doing my homework, when all at once, with only a rumble of warning . . .

down came the rain, *down* came the lightning, and all around and everywhere came the thunder."

"Wow," said Thomas. "What did you do?"

"Dove under the bed."

"But what about Melvin?"

"Well, I lay there shivering at every clap of thunder, and I'm ashamed to say that it was some time before I even remembered that my poor little dog was all by himself out in the storm."

"What did you *do?*" Thomas demanded.

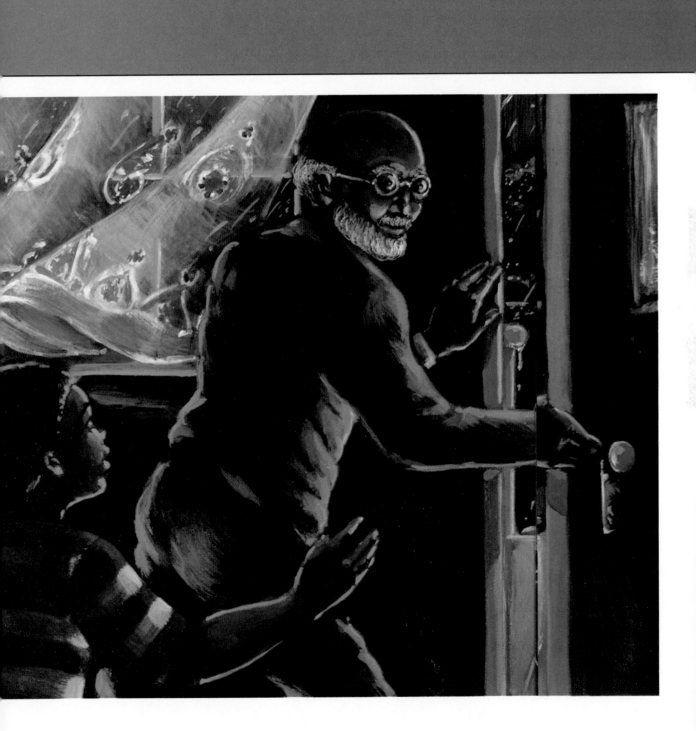

"Thomas—I put on my raincoat and opened the kitchen door and stepped out on the back porch just as a flash of lightning shook the whole sky and a clap of thunder barreled down and a huge man *appeared* out of the darkness, holding Melvin in his arms!"

"What's the end of the story?"

"Oh, just what you'd imagine," Grandfather said carelessly. "Having overcome my fear enough to forget myself and think about Melvin, I wasn't afraid of storms anymore."

"Grandfather?"

"Yes, Thomas?"

"What I think . . . I think that maybe if you hadn't been here, and Ringo hadn't been here, and I was all alone in the house and there was a storm and the lights went out and didn't come on again for a long time, like this . . . I think maybe *then* I would be a *little* bit afraid."

"Perfectly natural," said Grandfather.

After a while the lights came on.

They turned them off and went to bed.

Reader's Response

What did you like best about Grandfather's story?
What story would you tell on a stormy night?

Storm in the Night

📖 Responding to Literature

1. What did Thomas learn from Grandfather's story?

2. Remember a time when it was stormy? What sounds did you hear? Write a poem about the noises you hear during a thunderstorm.

3. What is your favorite way to spend a stormy night? Get together with friends and think up some good ideas.

📖 Books to Enjoy

Weather Forecasting by Gail Gibbons
Would you like to learn what people at the National Weather Service do? Then this is the book for you.

Flash, Crash, Rumble, and Roll by Franklyn M. Branley
The sounds of thunderstorms come alive in this book. Read it to find out about storms and how to stay safe during them.

HUMAN BODY

How Your Body Works

What would it be like if there were no clocks? How could you tell time? You might use clues, such as where the sun is in the sky. Scientists wonder how well the body tells time without clocks or clues.

Does the body know when to sleep? Does it know the right time to eat? To find out, this woman stayed in a cave deep underground. She had no clocks.

Strange things happened. Sometimes she would stay awake for 2 days. Then she would sleep for a whole night and day.

In this chapter you will learn what the parts of your body do. You will find out how these parts work together.

1. What do different body parts do?

Words to Know
brain
nerves

Getting Started Clap, kick, wink. Do each one. Which parts of the body do you use?

You cannot see all the parts of your body. Many parts are covered by skin, muscles, and bones. You can feel bones and muscles when you squeeze your arm or leg.

You can hear some body parts move. Sometimes you can hear your heart. Think about how your stomach makes noise. Listen as you tap your teeth.

Body parts work together. The girl's arm, hand, and eyes work together as she throws the disk. Think about the things you do. Your mouth, throat, and stomach work together when you eat and drink. What body parts work together when you read this book out loud?

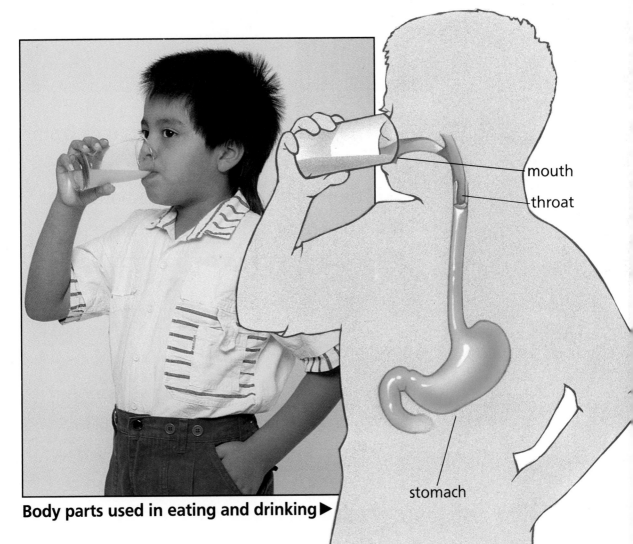

mouth

throat

stomach

Body parts used in eating and drinking ▶

brain

nerves

▲ **Body parts that carry messages**

Your **brain** controls many parts of the body. It does this by sending the body messages. **Nerves** carry these messages.

Your brain also gets messages from your body. Nerves carry those messages too. Your brain helps you find out what you taste, smell, hear, feel, and see. What other body parts help you do these things?

Lesson Review

1. Which body parts do you use to drink? Which do you use to throw a ball?
2. What do your brain and nerves do?

Think! Why is it very important to protect your head when you work or play?

THINKING

Skills

Learning by doing and watching

How do you learn a new game? A friend may help you to do the steps of the game. You could also watch other people playing the game. By watching them, you could find out how to play the game. You can learn from what you do and what you see.

Practice

Think about what it means to take a breath.

1. Sit in a chair. Sit up straight.
2. Place your hand above your stomach.
3. Take a deep breath. Watch your hand at the same time. How did your hand move? How did your stomach move?
4. Write what you did. Write what you saw.

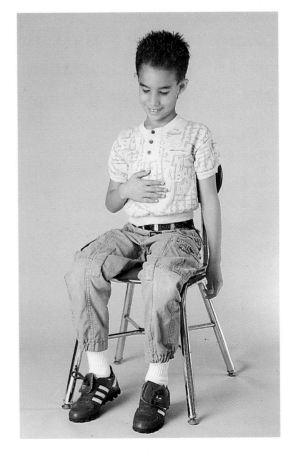

Apply

Put your hand on your neck. Feel your neck as you swallow. Write about what you felt.

2. How does your body move?

Words to Know

skeleton
bones
muscles
exercise

Getting Started How fast can you open and close your hand? What body parts move each time?

Your **skeleton** holds up your body. It also helps it move. All of the **bones** of your body make up your skeleton. Bones are hard body parts. They help give your body its shape. They also protect the parts inside your body. You can feel some of your large bones. You might even be able to count your ribs.

Some bones are too small to feel. You have about 30 bones in one arm and hand. You have over 200 bones in your skeleton!

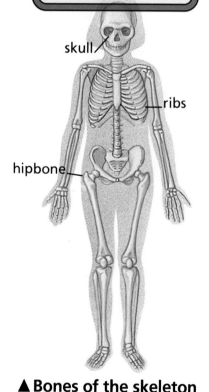

skull

ribs

hipbone

▲ Bones of the skeleton

260

Healthy bones grow. That is why you get taller. Healthy bones are strong bones. Eating healthful foods helps bones stay strong. Be careful when you play so you can keep bones from being injured.

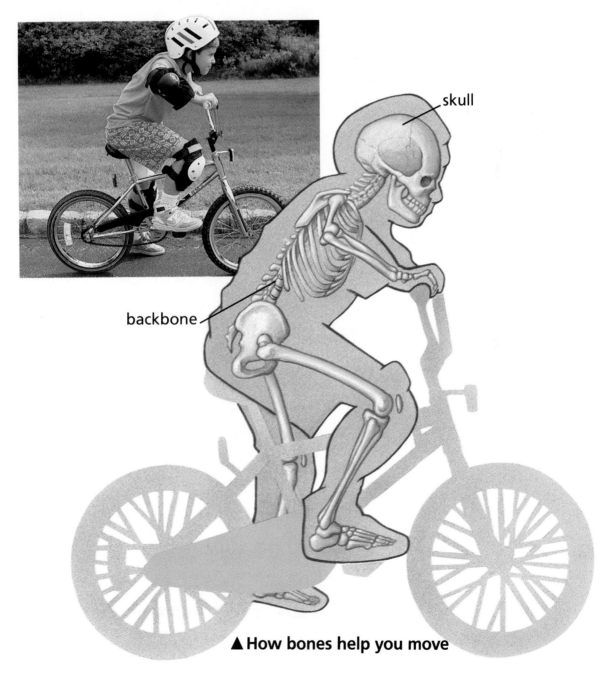

skull

backbone

▲ How bones help you move

this muscle
shortens

leg moves back

Bones do not move by themselves.
Muscles are body parts that help move
bones. Muscles are joined to bones.
Unlike bones, muscles are not hard.
Muscles change shape as you use them.
Muscles can get shorter or longer.

Look what happens when you kick
a ball. When one muscle gets shorter,
it pulls on the bone it is joined to. That
makes the bone move one way.

now this muscle shortens

leg moves forward

Another muscle pulls the bone the other way. Find this muscle in the drawing above. What happens to the bone when this muscle gets shorter?

Muscles can be large or small. Leg muscles are large. They help you run or walk. Face muscles are small. They let you smile or frown. They let you open and close your eyes. There are more than 600 muscles in your body.

Everyone should exercise. **Exercise** means moving your body to help make it stronger. Maybe you like to swim, dance, or run. You help build strong bones and muscles when you do these things. How are these people exercising?

Lesson Review

1. What do your bones do?
2. How can you help keep your bones healthy?
3. How do muscles help you move?

Think! What body part does your skull protect?

Explore

What does your backbone look like?

ACTIVITY

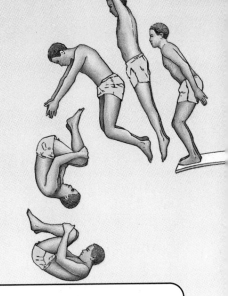

Your backbone is made of many small bones. Muscles work with these bones. They let you bend forward and backward. They let you turn from side to side.

You need

scissors • string • metric ruler • 2 plastic straws • tape

What to do

1. Cut two pieces of string. Each should be 30 centimeters long. **Be careful!** Scissors can cut you.
2. Pull one piece of string through a straw.
3. Cut the other straw into 1-centimeter pieces.

4. Pull the other piece of string through the small pieces of straw. Tape the ends.

What did you find out?

1. Which model can move more easily?
2. Which model is more like your backbone?

What is special about this hand?

Meet Katie. She loves to ride her bike. She swims, too. She is in a 4-H Club with her friends. Katie and her friends learn to take care of animals. Katie does many of these things using a special hand.

Katie was born with no left hand. She used to wear a metal hook on her arm. It helped her hold things. But when she was 5, she got her special hand. It is made of plastic.

STS

Katie's special hand has fingers like a real hand. Inside the fingers are metal rods. They have electricity in them. To move the fingers, Katie moves her arm muscles. The muscles send signals to the fingers. Then the fingers open or close.

Plastic hands like Katie's help a lot of people. They can do many things with their special hands.

Thinking about it

1. A plastic hand looks like a real hand. Is that important? Tell why or why not.

2. How is Katie like other children? What kinds of things does she do?

Using what you learned

Pretend you could help make a special hand for someone. What would it look like? What would it be able to do?

3. What happens when you exercise?

Words to Know
heart
oxygen

Getting Started What games give you the most exercise? How do you feel after you play these games?

Your heart pumps faster when you exercise. Your **heart** is a pump made of muscle. It pumps blood to all parts of your body. Find the swimmer's heart.

Blood carries two things that your body parts need. It carries food and oxygen. **Oxygen** is a gas in air. Your body gets oxygen when you breathe.

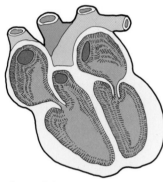

▲ Inside of heart

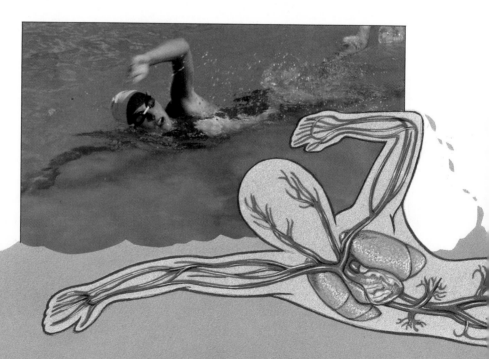

268

Your heart pumps between 80 and 90 times a minute. Every pump is one heartbeat. Every pump sends food and oxygen to all parts of your body.

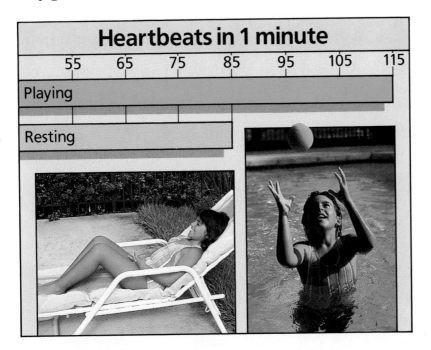

Heartbeats in 1 minute						
55	65	75	85	95	105	115

Playing

Resting

Suppose you are sitting still. Every time your heart beats you put a marble in a big bag. After just 2 hours the bag will be filled. Now suppose you are running. When you run fast or work hard, your heart beats faster. Then you would fill the bag even faster.

If Todd was going to win the race, he would have to train. Find out how he did it when you read **The Race** in Horizons Plus.

When you exercise, your muscles need a lot of food and oxygen. So do other body parts. That is why your heart beats faster.

When you exercise, your lungs work faster too. Have you ever played very hard? You get "out of breath." What does it feel like to be out of breath?

Rest also helps your body stay healthy. It is important to rest after you exercise. Rest also helps to keep your muscles and bones strong. It gives your bones a chance to grow. That is one reason why you need to get enough rest at night.

▲ Resting after exercising

Lesson Review

1. What does the heart do?
2. How does your body change when you are working or playing hard?
3. Why is rest important?

Think! What could you do to get your body ready for a long race?

271

Explore Together

What happens to your breathing rate after exercise?

You need

Planner timer • paper and pencil

What to do

Planner **1.** Sit in a chair for 1 minute.

Leader **2.** Count how many times the Planner breathes in the next minute.

Helper **3.** Tell the Leader when time is up.

Writer **4.** Write down the results.

Planner **5.** The Planner should jump in place for 1 minute. Then repeat steps **2** through **4**.

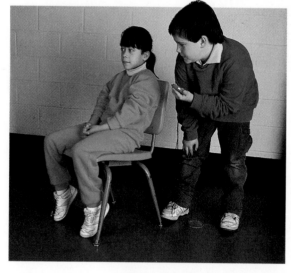 

What did you find out?

All, Writer **1.** How did the Planner's breathing change?

Reporter **2.** Share your results with the class.

Chapter 9 Putting It All Together

Chapter Connections

Copy this word map on a paper. Cut out the parts. Mix them up. Try to put them back together in the right order.

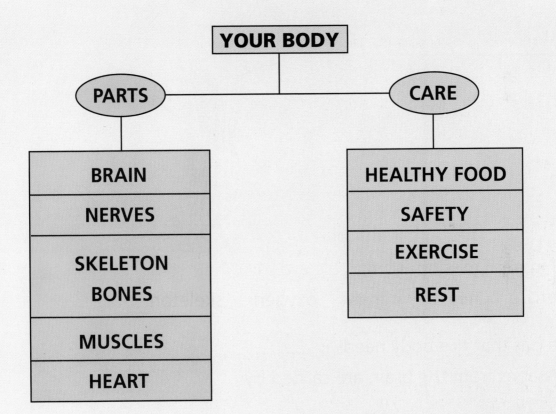

YOUR BODY

PARTS

- BRAIN
- NERVES
- SKELETON BONES
- MUSCLES
- HEART

CARE

- HEALTHY FOOD
- SAFETY
- EXERCISE
- REST

Writing About Science • Inform

Write a sentence about something people wear that keeps their body safe. Draw a picture to go with the sentence.

Science Words

A. Match each word with a body part.

bone   brain   muscle

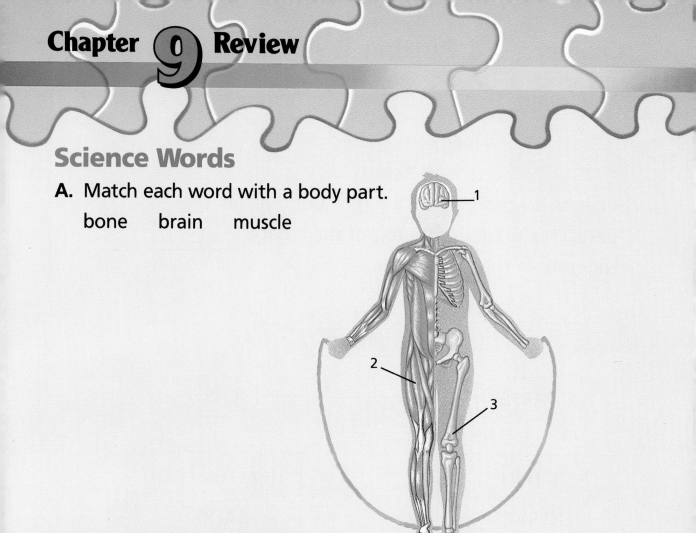

B. Fill in each missing word.

exercise   heart   nerves   oxygen   skeleton

1. The gas that the body needs is _____.

2. Messages from the brain are carried by
_____.

3. All the bones of your body are called the
_____.

4. You make your body stronger when you
_____.

5. The muscle that pumps blood is the _____.

Science Ideas

1. What are some body parts that you cannot see?
2. What do the brain and nerves do?
3. What does the skeleton do?
4. What are two things that your bones do?
5. How do muscles work together with bones?
6. What happens to a bone when a muscle joined to it gets shorter?
7. What is exercise?
8. What happens to your heart when you exercise?

Applying Science Ideas

Suppose your friend is born with only one hand. How might a special hand help your friend?

Using Science Skills

Put your hand on your jaw. Move your mouth as if you are chewing. Write to tell what moves as you chew.

Chapter 10

Keeping Your Body Safe

This rubber suit was made over 100 years ago. It was used like a lifeboat. The top of the suit opened wide so that it could be put on quickly. Food and water were stored inside the suit. A tube at the top brought in fresh air. The suit could save someone who was on a sinking boat.

These girls are wearing something used for water safety. Other things are used for water safety also. What kinds of water safety things have you used?

In this chapter you will learn about safety at home and at school. You will learn many ways to keep yourself and others safe.

1. How can you be safe at home?

Words to Know
poison
smoke detector

Getting Started   Some things should not be touched by babies or young children. Make a sign using pictures to say "Do not touch." What things at home can you put your sign on?

These children are making the house safe for the baby. They are picking up little objects. They do not want the baby to swallow something and choke.

They do not want the baby to touch something sharp. Why must you be careful with a baby in the house?

▼ Putting away toys

278

▲ Putting away harmful things

PAINT REMOVER

NO METHYLENE CHLORIDE   HEAVY DUTY SEMI-PASTE
WORKS FOR HOURS, WILL NOT DRY OUT
DISSOLVES ALL PAINTS & FINISHES
EXCEPTIONAL POLYURETHANE VARNISH & LACQUER REMOVER
EASY WATER WASH   REMOVES STAIN

DANGER-POISON
KEEP OUT OF REACH OF CHILDREN. MAY BE FATAL IF SWALLOWED.
ONE PINT (.473 LITERS)

▲ Poison sign on bottle

Young children like to put things into their mouths. But they might eat or drink something with poison in it. **Poison** can hurt them.

The family moves all bottles and cans with poison in them to a high shelf. Then a young child cannot reach them. How can you tell when a bottle has something harmful in it?

Fire can be very harmful. You should know how to prevent fire. You should also know what to do in case a fire happens in your home.

◄Have a working smoke detector. A **smoke detector** makes a loud noise when smoke from a fire reaches it. The battery should be changed every year.

Do not play with matches or fire of any kind. If you find matches, give them to a parent.▼

Have a plan to get out of your house if it is on fire. Practice fire drills with your family.▶

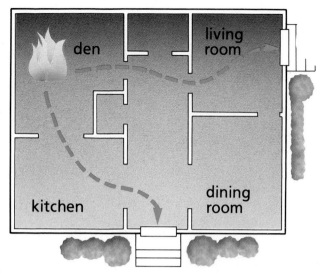

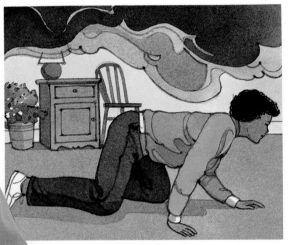

◀In a fire, get out fast. Smoke rises to the ceiling. The smoke is very harmful. Crawl on hands and knees to stay under the smoke.

Choose a place outside to meet your family. Do not go back inside a burning building.▶

Look at how this man is carrying the clippers. The sharp ends are pointing down. This is the safe way to carry sharp tools.

This man is trying to make the garage a safe place. He will put the clippers where children cannot reach them. Tools can cause harm if they are not stored or used the right way.

▲ Putting away tools

Lesson Review

1. Why is it unsafe for children to put small objects into their mouths?
2. What can a family do to protect itself from fire?
3. How should sharp tools be carried?

Think! How can you make your home safer?

THINKING

Skills

Asking what is happening

Sometimes you see things. You want to know about them. Then you can ask questions. Maybe you want to know why some bottles are so hard to open. To find out, you can ask why.

Practice

Look at the picture. It shows a woman building a table. What do you want to know about what is happening? What question can you ask so that you can tell what is happening? Do you wonder about safety? What else do you want to know? Write some questions about the picture.

Apply

Think about safety rules in your school. Write a question about school safety.

2. How can you play safely?

Words to Know

rules

Getting Started Make a list of the games you like to play. How do you keep safe when you play each one?

Games have rules. **Rules** tell people how to play a game. A game is more fun when everyone follows the rules.

Some game rules help to keep the players safe. Sometimes the rules let players rest before they get too tired. Think about the games you play. What rules keep you safe?

It is important to follow the rules when you play games and sports. That is why your family and your school have rules about how you can play.

These children are skating and playing ball the right way. They wear certain things that help keep them safe. What is each child wearing? How do these things help keep the children safe? On pages 276 and 277 you saw something worn for water safety.

Sometimes people need to be told again about the safety rules. Signs help them.

Look at the children swimming. They are each swimming with a friend. They know it is not safe to swim alone. There is a sign by the pool to remind them of the rules. Why is it a good thing to follow the rules when swimming?

POOL RULES & REGULATIONS

POOL HOURS: 9 A.M. to 11 P.M.

A – SMALL POOL IS FOR BABYS UP TO 4 YEARS OLD ONLY.
B – CHILDREN 12 YEARS OLD & UNDER MUST BE SUPERVISED BY AN ADULT.
C – CHILDREN WITH DIAPERS ARE NOT ALLOWED IN ANY POOL.
D – BALLS, FLOATS, RAFTS & DIVING EQUIPMENT ARE NOT ALLOWED IN THE POOL OR POOL AREA.
E – NO BICYCLES, SKATEBOARDS OR ROLLER SKATES ARE ALLOWED IN THE POOL AREA.
F – SHOWER BEFORE ENTERING POOL FROM THE BEACH.
G – NO ANIMALS ALLOWED IN THE POOL OR POOL AREA.
H – NO GLASSWARE, FOOD OR DRINKS ALLOWED IN POOL OR POOL AREA.
I – DO NOT REMOVE LOUNGE CHAIRS FROM POOL AREA.
J – PERSONS WITH INFECTIOUS DISEASES OR OPEN WOUNDS ARE NOT ALLOWED IN THE POOL.
K – NO DIVING, PUSHING OR RUNNING ALLOWED.
L – NO HIGH VOLUME RADIOS ALLOWED IN POOL AREA.
M – KEEP POOL AREA CLEAN.
N – KEEP ALL APT. DOORS CLOSED... PLEASE.

NO LIFEGUARD ON DUTY • SWIM AT YOUR OWN RISK

Board of Directors

Lesson Review

1. Why are rules important?
2. What are three safety rules that help to keep people safe when they are playing?

Think! Why is it safer to always go swimming with another person?

ACTIVITY

Explore Together

How can you play safely in a playground?

You need

Planner   paper • markers • posterboard

What to do

Leader **1.** Ask your teacher if you and your group can take a tour of a nearby playground.

Helper **2.** Tell all the things that are in the playground.

Writer **3.** Draw a picture of the playground.

All **4.** Think about the safe ways to use the playground. Think of safety rules.

Writer **5.** Write down the safety rules.

What did you find out?

All, Writer **1.** Will the safety rules affect how you play?

Reporter **2.** Explain your safety rules to others.

3. How can you travel safely?

Words to Know
seatbelt

Getting Started How many different ways have you traveled?

There are many ways to get from place to place. You can walk or ride a bicycle. You can ride in a car, bus, train, or airplane. The rules to follow when you travel help keep you safe.

Think about ways to be safe in a car. You should get into and out of the car on the side next to the curb. You should always wear your seatbelt. A **seatbelt** holds you in your seat. What other rules should you follow?

These children ride a bus to and from school. The children are very careful. They do not stand too close to the curb while they are waiting.

When the school bus stops, lights on the bus will flash. These lights warn other traffic to stop. Then the children can cross the street to go home.

Some children ride bicycles to school. Do you like to ride a bicycle? Here are some ways to ride safely.

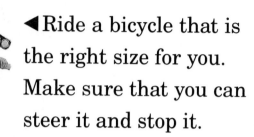

◄Ride a bicycle that is the right size for you. Make sure that you can steer it and stop it.

Check your bicycle to be sure that it is safe. A flag will help people see you. Never ride in the dark. Wear a helmet.►

◄Obey all traffic signals. Do what the lights and signs tell you to do.

Pick a safe route. Stay away from busy traffic. Let people know where you are going. Use hand signals.▼

Right turn

Left turn

Stop

Ride single file when you are with friends. Stay on the same side of the street.▶

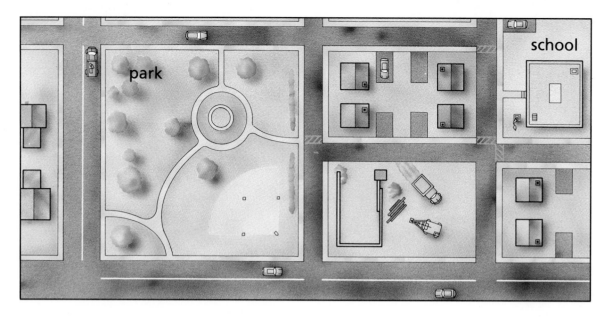

This map shows part of a town. There are crosswalks to show you where to cross. At crosswalks the lights and signs help keep you safe.

Learn to ride a bicycle safely. Read **The Bear's Bicycle**, page 306.

Plan a walk or a bike ride from your home to the park. Think about the safest way you can go. Look for streets with sidewalks. Plan where to cross.

Lesson Review ▬▬▬▬

1. How can you travel safely by car?

2. What is one safety rule for taking the school bus to and from school?

3. What are two rules for bicycle safety?

Think! What is the safest way to walk from your house to school?

Explore

How do seatbelts keep us safe?

Safety experts tell us that "Seatbelts Save Lives." Find out why seatbelts are important for safety.

You need

toy person • toy car • rubber bands • 3 books • board •

What to do

1. Put a toy person in a toy car. Use rubber bands for the seatbelt.
2. Make a ramp with books and a board.
3. Roll the car down the ramp. Let it hit a wall. Watch what happens.
4. Take off the seatbelt. Repeat step **3**.

What did you find out?

1. What happened when there was a seatbelt?
2. What happened when there was no seatbelt?
3. Why are seatbelts important?

4. How can you be safe on your own?

Getting Started Have you ever been alone or away from family or friends? How did you feel? What did you do?

Know what to do when you are on your own. Never tell anyone over the phone if you are home alone. Do not open the door to a stranger. A **stranger** is someone you do not know.

Know how to act if you meet a stranger on the street. Never give your name, address, or phone number to a stranger. If someone asks you for directions, you should walk away.

If a stranger offers you candy or money, you should walk away. If the stranger is in a car, you should walk or run away. If you are really scared, then scream.

You should have a plan in case a stranger bothers you. Know where to go if you need help. Go into a store. Ask the people there for help.

The best plan is not to be alone. Try to go places with a friend. Who in the picture is doing the safe thing?

You should know what a good touch is and what a bad touch is. A good touch makes you feel happy. A bad touch may frighten you or make you feel strange. If someone touches you and says to keep it a secret, tell a parent.

People at school can help too. Do not be afraid to ask for help.

▲ You can ask a teacher for help.

No one should be hurt by another person. No one has the right to make you do something that does not feel right.

Do not let a stranger touch you. If a stranger tries to touch you shout, "I don't know you!" Get away from that person. Tell your parents or a teacher about that person.

◄ Good touches can make you feel happy.

Know what to do if you are lost. If you are on the street, look for a store. If you do not see one, look for the police. Tell them you need help.

If you are lost in a big store, find someone who works there. Tell them you need help. Do not leave the store.

Or find a pay phone. Dial "O" to get the Operator. You can do this for free from many pay phones. Tell the Operator that you are lost. Tell where you are calling from.

Drugs can be good or bad. Good drugs can help you. If you are sick, your parents or a doctor may give you these drugs. The drugs can make you feel better. Never take drugs on your own.

Bad drugs harm your body. They are against the law. If someone offers you these drugs, do not take them. Say "No" and walk away.

Lesson Review

1. What should you do if a stranger talks to you?

2. Who can help you if you are lost?

Think! A stranger asks you to help her find her lost puppy. What should you do?

Problem Solving

Stick Together

There are safe ways to do things. Think about walking home from school. It is safer to walk with a friend than to walk alone. Many things you do are safer when you use the buddy system. Using the buddy system means doing things with friends, parents, brothers, or sisters.

How can the buddy system keep you safe?

Look at the picture carefully. What do you think is happening in this picture? How could the girl in the picture be safer?

Chapter Connections

List three more things that could be put in this word map.

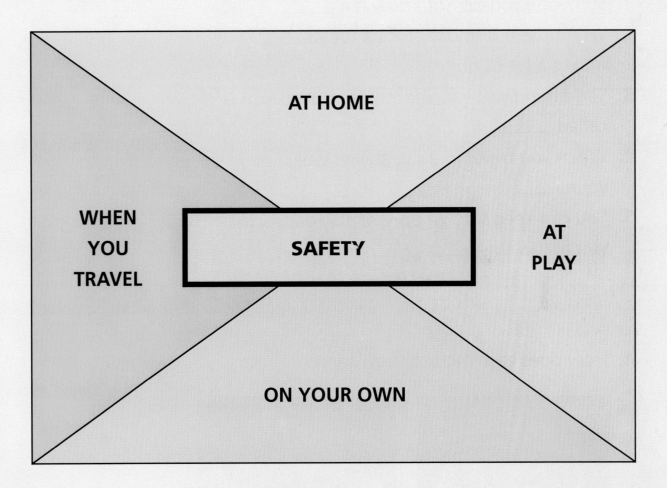

AT HOME

WHEN YOU TRAVEL

SAFETY

AT PLAY

ON YOUR OWN

Writing About Science • Research

Find out about safety rules at your school.
Write three safety rules you follow at school.

Science Words

Fill in each missing word.

poison   rules   seatbelt   smoke detector   stranger

1. Someone you do not know is a _____.
2. When there is smoke from a fire, a _____ makes a lot of noise.
3. Something you eat or drink that hurts you is called _____.
4. When you travel in a car, always wear your _____.
5. You can keep safe when you play games if you follow the _____.

Science Ideas

1. How does each picture show safety?

a  b

c PAINT REMOVER

N3 METHYLENE CHLORIDE HEAVY DUTY SEMI-PASTE

WORKS FOR HOURS,
WILL NOT DRY OUT

DISSOLVES
ALL PAINTS
& FINISHES

EXCEPTIONAL
POLYURETHANE VARNISH
& LACQUER REMOVER

EASY WATER WASH REMOVES STAIN

DANGER-POISON
KEEP OUT OF REACH OF
CHILDREN. MAY BE FATAL
IF SWALLOWED.

ONE PINT (.473 LITERS)

2. How are game rules helpful?

3. What should you do if a stranger asks you for directions?

Applying Science Ideas

When might you or a friend need to talk to a police officer?

Using Science Skills

Look at the picture. People use these things when they play sports. Ask some safety questions about these things.

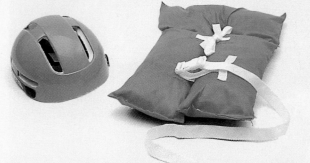

Careers

Movement Teacher

Liz Collins is a **movement teacher**. She works in a hospital in New Jersey. Liz helps children who have been hurt. Some of the children do not have arms or legs. They must learn to use plastic arms or legs.

At first these children cannot do many things. Liz teaches them to move. They learn how to wash, dress, eat, and play.

Liz went to college to learn about the human body. "I love to help kids," says Liz.

Connecting Science Ideas

1. You read about a girl named Katie who has a plastic hand. How do you think a movement teacher helped her? **Careers; Chapter 9**

2. You learned what your brain does. How can you keep your brain safe when you play? **Chapter 9; Chapter 10**

3. You read about keeping safe in water. The best way is to know how to swim! What body parts do you use to swim? **Chapter 9; Chapter 10**

4. What are some ways to exercise? Where are some safe places for children to exercise? **Chapter 9; Chapter 10**

5. What body parts could be hurt if a baby eats poison? **Chapter 9; Chapter 10**

Unit Project

You learned about fire safety. Make a safety checklist in case of fire. Tell how each person will get out of your home. Decide where your family will meet outside. What else should be in your fire safety plan?

from
The Bear's Bicycle

by

EMILIE WARREN McLEOD

Illustrated by

DAVID McPHAIL

Do you know how to ride a bicycle safely?
Bear doesn't! Luckily a friend shows him how.

Every afternoon we go bike riding.
I check the tires and the brakes and
make sure the handlebars turn.

If I have to cross the street I stop and get off my bike.

I look both ways.

If no cars are coming I walk my bike across the street.

I watch for car doors that are open.

And when I come up behind people I warn them
so they can get out of the way.

I always start home before it is dark and put away my bike.
I wipe my feet before going in the house.
Then we have milk and crackers.

Reader's Response

When you go out to play, what do you
do to keep safe?

The Bear's Bicycle

📖 Responding to Literature

1. Name some safe places to ride a bicycle in your neighborhood. Name some places that are not safe. Talk to your friends about your ideas.

2. What might happen if bicycle riders do not follow the rules?

3. Make a poster that shows rules bicycle riders should follow.

📖 Books to Enjoy

What's the Matter, Sylvie, Can't You Ride?
by Karen Born Andersen
Learning to ride a bike is hard! Just when Sylvie is ready to give up, something happens. If you like bikes, you will like this story.

Dinosaurs Beware! A Safety Guide
by Marc Brown and Stephen Krensky
A funny group of dinosaurs learns about safety.

Glossary

A

absorbed   What happens to light that strikes an object and is trapped by the object. More light is absorbed by dark colors than by light colors. page 150

air   A mix of many gases. You cannot see air, but you can feel it move. page 196

amphibian   An animal that lives part of its life in water and part on land. An amphibian has thin, wet skin. page 48

B

balance   A tool that shows which of two objects has the most matter. A balance works like a seesaw. page 132

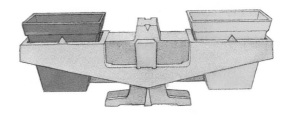

bird   An animal that has wings and a beak. All birds lay eggs. page 38

body covering   The outer part of an animal that helps protect the animal. The body covering of a bird is feathers. page 34

bones   Hard body parts that help give the body its shape. Bones also protect the parts inside the body. page 260

brain   The body part that controls many other body parts. The brain sends messages to other body parts. page 258

breeze   A wind that moves gently. You may see leaves flutter when there is a breeze. page 231

C

clouds   Tiny drops of liquid water or bits of ice that float in air. Rain or snow may fall from clouds. page 234

cone   A plant part in which seeds form. Pine trees have cones. page 60

D

dinosaur   Animals that lived millions of years ago. All dinosaurs lived on land. page 84

E

electricity   A form of energy used for light, heat, and to run machines. In a toaster, electricity is changed to heat. page 144

endangered   May become extinct. Whooping cranes are endangered birds. page 101

energy What is needed to change things or make things move. Light, sound, and heat are forms of energy. page 140

exercise Moving your body to help make it stronger. Swimming, dancing, and running are kinds of exercise. page 264

extinct All animals of one kind die. There are no dinosaurs today because these animals are extinct. page 90

F

fish An animal that lives and breathes under water. Most fish are covered with scales. page 42

flower A plant part in which seeds form. Part of a flower may grow into a fruit. page 60

fog A cloud that is close to the ground. If you walk through fog, you are inside a cloud. page 237

fossils Clues about living things of long ago. Dinosaur footprints in rock are one kind of fossil. page 95

friction The rubbing together of two things that causes heat. When you rub your hands together fast, you can feel heat from friction. page 154

fuel   Something that is burned to give heat. Oil, gas, wood, and coal are kinds of fuel. page 154

G

gas   A form of matter that does not have a shape. A gas spreads out to fill what it is in. page 124

gust   A short burst of strong wind. People need to hold on to their hats when there is a gust. page 231

H

heart   A pump in the body that is made of muscle. Your heart pumps blood to all parts of your body. page 268

heat   A form of energy used to change matter. Heat is used to warm homes. page 142

I

insect   An animal with six legs. The body of an insect has a hard covering. page 50

L

length   How long something is. The length of an object can be measured in centimeters. page 130

light   A form of energy you can see. The sun and the stars give off light. page 141

liquid   A form of matter that does not have its own shape. When a liquid is put into a jar, it takes the shape of the jar. page 123

M

mammal   An animal that gets milk from its mother's body. Most mammals have fur or hair. page 36

mass   A measure of how much matter there is in an object. Mass is measured in grams. page 133

matter   What all things are made of. All matter takes up space. page 120

meat eater   An animal that eats only other animals. Dinosaurs that were meat eaters had sharp pointed teeth. page 88

mollusk   An animal with a soft body. A snail is a mollusk that has a hard shell covering its body. page 44

muscles   Body parts that help to move bones. Muscles get shorter when they are used. page 262

N

nerves   Body parts that carry messages to and from the brain. Nerves carry messages about what you taste, smell, hear, feel, and see.   page 258

O

oxygen   One of the gases in air. Plants and animals must have oxygen to live. page 196, page 268

P

plant eater   An animal that eats only plants. Some dinosaurs were plant eaters.   page 87

poison   Something that can hurt the body. A bottle that has poison in it must be kept on a high shelf. page 279

pollen   The part of a flower that is needed to make tiny eggs in a flower grow into seeds. Some pollen looks like bits of yellow dust. page 61

pollute   To make water, land, or air dirty. The burning of leaves pollutes the air.   page 100, page 212

R

recycle   To use over and over again. People recycle glass, paper, and metal cans. page 215

reflected   What happens to light that hits something and then bounces off. Almost all the light that hits a mirror is reflected. page 149

reptile   An animal that has scaly skin. Most reptiles lay eggs that have thick shells. page 46

rotate   To spin. The earth rotates once in about 24 hours. page 183

rules   What tells people how to play a game or sport. Some game rules help to keep the players safe. page 284

S

season   A time of the year. Spring, summer, fall, and winter are the seasons. page 74

seatbelt   Something that holds you in your seat when you ride in a car. You should always wear your seatbelt in a car. page 288

seed coat   The hard covering of a seed. The seed coat protects the seed. page 70

shadow   A dark shape formed when an object blocks light. Shadows can become longer or shorter. page 188

skeleton   The bones of the body that hold up the body and help it move. Scientists have found dinosaur skeletons. page 96, page 260

smoke detector
Something that makes a loud noise when smoke from a fire reaches it. You should have a working smoke detector. page 280

solid   A form of matter that has its own shape. When a solid is put into a jar, the shape of the solid stays the same. page 122

sound   A form of energy you can hear. Sound energy moves through all kinds of matter. page 143

spider   An animal with eight legs. The body of a spider has a hard covering. page 52

sprout   To start to grow. A seed sprouts when the tiny plant inside the seed breaks through the seed coat. page 71

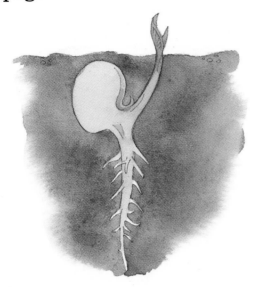

star   An object in the sky that gives off light. The sun is a star. page 178

storm   Weather that has very strong winds. Storms can cause high waves along shores. page 232

stranger   Someone you do not know. Do not open the door to a stranger. page 294

sun   The star that is closest to the earth. The sun is a huge ball of burning gases. page 178

T

temperature   How hot or cold something is. The temperature of the air can be measured. page 226

thermometer   A tool that measures temperature. Most thermometers use numbers to show the temperature. page 227

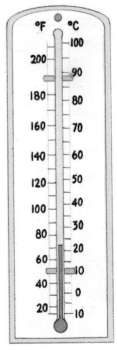

V

vibrate   When an object moves back and forth. Sound energy comes from things that vibrate. page 158

volume   The space that matter takes up. The volume of matter can be measured in milliliters. page 131

W

water vapor   Water that is a gas. You cannot see water vapor. page 126, page 200

weather   What the air outside is like. If the air changes, the weather changes. page 222

wind vane   A tool that shows where the wind is coming from. You can see a wind vane on the roof of some houses. page 230

Index

Credits

Front Cover, Title Page: © Peter B. Kaplan/Photo Researchers, Inc.; **Back Cover:** Nicholas de Vore III/Bruce Coleman.

Contributing Artists: Joanne Adams: 260, 262, 263; Ernest Albanese: 129; Suzanne Clee: 55–57, 79–81, 105–107, 135–137, 164–165, 191–193, 218–219, 242–243, 301–303. Kathy Deeter: 66, 67, 70, 71, 74–77, 80; Len Ebert: 78, 199, 233, 281, 293; David Germon: 155, 162, 269, 280; Grace Goldberg: 13, 45; John Hamberger: 40, 49, 50, 54, 95, 104; Douglas Henderson: 82–83; Harvo Ishioko: 178, 179, 184; Phil Jones: 265; Joe LeMonnier: 207, 281, 292; Jeff Mangiat: 288, 289; Davis Meltzer: 84–88, 90–92; James Needham: 17, 21, 43, 48, 49, 51, 54; Dennis O'Brien: 276; Mike Radencich: 226, 227, 234, 235; Judy Reed: 229; Nancy Schill: 81, 219; Samantha Smith: 162, 218, 300; Kate Sweeney: 257, 258, 260, 261, 268, 269, 274; Arthur Thompson: 186–187. Glossary: Nancy Schill

Photographs
All photographs by Silver Burdett & Ginn (SB&G) unless otherwise noted.

Table of Contents: 4: Kamyar Samoul; 6: Yuri Doje/Image Bank; 8: © Phil Jude/Photo Researchers, Inc.; 10: David Madison.

Introductory Chapter 14–15: Arnoldo Mondadori Editore, SpA., Milan; 14, 17, 22, 24, 26, 27, 28: Peter Menzel/Dinamation International Corporation. 16: Nick Rochester/The Morris Museum, Morristown, NJ. 20, 25: John Lei/OPC for SB&G.

Unit 1 opener 29: Kamyar Samoul

Chapter 1 30–31: Animals Animals/© Stephen Dalton. 32: *m.l.* Animals Animals/R.F. Head; *b.m.* Chris Baker/TSW–Click, Chicago. 33: *t.l.* E.R. Degginger; *t.m.* Runk-Schoenberger/Grant Heilman Photography; *t.r.* Ed Rescher/Peter Arnold, Inc.; *m., b.r.* E.R. Degginger; *m.l.* Paul L. Janosi/Valan Photos. 34: *m.l.* Dan DeWilde for SB&G; *m.* Animals Animals/Robert Maier; *m.r.* Hans Reinhard/Bruce Coleman; *b.l.* Bruce Coleman. 36: *t.* C.C. Lockwood; *b.* Animals Animals/ Stephen Dalton. 37: *t.* Erwin & Peggy Bauer; *m.* E.R. Degginger; *b.* Jeff Foott. 38: *t.l.* © Charles W. Mann/Photo Researchers, Inc.; *t.r.* Jeff Foott; *b.* Murray O'Neill/Valan Photos. 38–39: *b.* J.A. Wilkinson/Valan Photos. 39: *t.* E.R. Degginger; *m.* Rod Planck/TOM STACK & ASSOCIATES; *b.* Guy Lebel/Valan Photos. 40: *m.* TSW/Click, Chicago. 41: *l.* John Colwell/Grant Heilman Photography; *r.* Grant Heilman Photography; *b.* Steve Maka for SB&G. 43: *t.* Carl Roessler/TSW– Click, Chicago; *b.* E.R. Degginger. 44: *m.l.* © J.H. Robinson/Photo Researchers, Inc.; *b.l.* Townsend P. Dickinson/Comstock; *t.m., b.m., t.r.* © James Carmichael/Photo Researchers, Inc.; *m., t.l.* © L. West/Photo Researchers, Inc.; *b.r.* © J.H. Robinson/Photo Researchers, Inc. 46: *m.* Dan DeWilde for SB&G. 47: *t.r.* Animals Animals/Zig Leszczynski; *m.l.* Breck P. Kent; *b.* Kennon Cooke/Valan Photos. 48: *b.l.* Animals Animals/Breck P. Kent; *b.r.* © L. & D. Klein/Photo Researchers, Inc. 49: *m.r.* Aubrey Lang/Valan Photos. 51: *b.l.* John Fowler/Valan Photos; *b.r.* Grant Heilman Photography. 52: *t.* Animals Animals/Ted Levin; *m.r.* © Laurence Pringle/Photo Researchers, Inc.; *b.* S.J. Krasemann/Peter Arnold, Inc. 53: *t.r.* Dick George /TOM STACK & ASSOCIATES; *m.l.* Animals Animals/Jim Bockowski; *b.r.* Milton Rand/TOM STACK & ASSOCIATES. 54: Dan DeWilde for SB&G.

Chapter 2 58–59: Grant Heilman Photography. 61: Hans Pfletschinger/Peter Arnold, Inc. 62: *t.l.* Avril Ramage/Oxford Scientific Labs/Earth Scenes; *m.l.* Larry Lefever/Grant Heilman Photography; *m.r.* Runk-Schoenberger/Grant Heilman Photography. 63: *m.l.* John Colwell/Grant Heilman Photography; *m.r.* Thomas Kitchin/TOM STACK & ASSOCIATES. 64: P.W. Simon/USDA/ University of Wisconsin. 65: *b.l.* Fritz Prenzel/Peter Arnold, Inc.; *b.r.* Jeanne Heiberg/Peter Arnold, Inc.; *m.l.* © Joyce Photographics/Photo Researchers, Inc.; *m.* Ted Levin/Earth Scenes; *m.r.* © Bill Bachman/Photo Researchers, Inc. 66: Carlye Calvin; 67: *t.l.* E.R. Degginger; *b.r.* Mia & Klaus/ SuperStock. 70: *b.r.* Barry L. Runk/Grant Heilman Photography. 71: Barry L. Runk/Grant Heilman Photography. 72: *t.l., m.r.* John Colwell/Grant Heilman Photography; *m.l.* Animals Animals/Earth Scenes/E.R. Degginger. 73: *m.r.* Dwight R. Kuhn; *b.r.* Frank Siteman for SB&G; *m.l.* Stephen Maka for SB&G. 74: © Joyce Photographics/Photo Researchers, Inc. 75: *m.l.* Mary E. Messenger; *b.r.* Phil & Loretta Hermann/TOM STACK & ASSOCIATES. 76: Don & Pat Valenti/ TOM STACK & ASSOCIATES. 77: © David Stoecklein/The Stock Market.

Chapter 3 93: Light Mechanics for SB&G. 94: Grant Heilman Photography. 95: *t.l.* E.R. Degginger; *m.* Sullivan & Rogers/Bruce Coleman. 96: *t.l.* Breck P. Kent; *b.* Keith Gunnar/Bruce Coleman. 97: *l.* American Museum of Natural History; *r.* Carnegie Museum of Natural History. 98: *t.* Michael Khun; *b.* Ray Nelson/Phototake, NYC. 99: Michael Khun. 100: *b.r.* Claudio Ferrer/TSW– Click, Chicago; *b.l.* Gary Milburn/TOM STACK & ASSOCIATES. 101: *t.l.* Frank Lanting; *b.l.*

Animals Animals/Jim Tuten; *t.r.* Jo-Ann Ordano; *b.l.* Jeff Foott. 102–103: Tom Mangelsen/Images of Nature. 102: *b.l.* W. Perry Conway/TOM STACK & ASSOCIATES; *b.r.* Tom Mangelsen/Images of Nature. 103: *l.* Tom Mangelsen/Images of Nature; *b.r.* Wendy Latill & Bob Rozinski/TOM STACK & ASSOCIATES. 108: Courtesy of Peggy Bechtel.

Unit 2 opener   117: Yuri Dojc/Image Bank.

Chapter 4   118–119: Ken Karp Photography for SB&G. 124: *b.l.* IMAGERY. 126–127: *b.* David Lissy/Leo deWys, Inc. 127: *l.* © D. Spindel/SuperStock; *r.* © Rick Altman/The Stock Market. 128: *t.* D. Winston/H. Armstrong Roberts.

Chapter 5   138–139: © Robert Goldwitz/Photo Researchers, Inc.; *b.* Mark Segal/Panoramic Stock Images. 140–141: © Piotr Kapa/The Stock Market. 141: *t.r.* Animals Animals/James E. Lloyd; *b.r.* Comstock. 143: *m.l.* © J. Barry O'Rourke/The Stock Market; *b.r.* Dan DeWilde for SB&G. 146: Patrick Riviere/Phototake, NYC. 147: G.M. Hughs Electronics. 148–149: © Sonya Jacobs/The Stock Market. 149: Rick Rusing/After Image, Inc. 150: Richard Haynes for SB&G. 154: *t.* Elizabeth Crews/Stock, Boston. 156: *t.r.* Teri Gilman/After Image, Inc. 157: *t.r., l.* Dwight R. Kuhn; *b.r.* Light Mechanics for SB&G. 159 *t.* James H. Karales/Peter Arnold, Inc.; *b.* Animals Animals/Bruce A. McDonald. 160: John Lei/OPC. 161: © Pete Saloutos/After Image, Inc. 166: Darwin Dale for SB&G.

Unit 3 opener: 175: © Phil Jude/Photo Researchers, Inc.

Chapter 6   176–177: Yoav Levy/Phototake, NYC. 179: © Jerry Schad/Science Source/Photo Researchers, Inc. 180: David Muench/AllStock, Inc. 181: *l.* Frank Siteman for SB&G; *r.b.* Light Mechanics for SB&G. 182: L. West/Bruce Coleman. 184: Hershkowitz-Kaplan/Bruce Coleman. 186: *b.l.* Dan DeWilde for SB&G. 187: Dan DeWilde for SB&G. 189: Pete Saloutos/After Image, Inc. 190: Richard Haynes for SB&G.

Chapter 7   194–195: Frans Lanting/Minden Pictures. 196: Ron Dahlquist/After Image, Inc. 197: *t.* Fred Bavendam/AllStock, Inc.; *b.* Ken Karp/OPC for SB&G. 198: © J.P. Ferrero-Jacana/Photo Researchers, Inc. 199: Ken Karp/OPC for SB&G. 200: *t.* NASA; *b.l.* Ken Karp/OPC for SB&G. 201: *t.r.* Comstock; *m.l.* Jim Corwin; *b.r.* © Pete Saloutos/The Stock Market. 202: Comstock. 203: Ken Karp for SB&G. 204: © 1991 Woodfin Camp & Associates. 204–205: David Hiser/Photographers/Aspen. 206: *t.* Collier-Condit/Stock, Boston; *b.* Rich Wasaki. 207: Galen Rowell/Peter Arnold, Inc. 208: Ken Karp/OPC for SB&G. 209: *l.* Ed Simpson/After Image, Inc.; *b.* © Richard Hutchings/Photo Researchers, Inc. 210: Comstock. 211: Frank Siteman for SB&G. 212: *l.* Ken Biggs/After Image, Inc.; *r.* Martha Cooper/Peter Arnold, Inc. 213: *t.* Mark Lewis/After Image, Inc.; *b.l.* Gary Braasch/AllStock, Inc./Alaska Photo Collection; *b.r.* Fred Bavendam/Peter Arnold, Inc. 214: Michal Heron. 215: *l.* Mark Antman/The Image Works; *r.* © Andrew Rakoczy/Photo Researchers, Inc. 216: Ken Karp/OPC for SB&G.

Chapter 8   220–221: Clyde H. Smith/Peter Arnold, Inc. 221: Myron Ace. 222: John Lei/Stock, Boston. 223: *l.* Jean Claude le Jeune/Stock, Boston; *r.* © Dave Driscoll/Photo Researchers, Inc. 224: Animals Animals/Earth Scenes/Richard Kolar. 225: John Curtis/Offshoot for SB&G. 227: *b.l., b.r.* Carlye Calvin. 228: *t.* Michal Heron. 230: *l.* Lincoln Russell/Stock, Boston; *b.* Daniel Brody/Stock, Boston. 230–231: *r.* Animals Animals/Earth Scenes/Ralph A. Reinhold; *m.* David R. Frazier Photolibrary, Inc. 232: *m.* © 1991 J.B. Diederich/Woodfin Camp & Associates; *t., m., b.* Edi Ann Otto. 235: *t.* © 1991 Sepp Seitz/Woodfin Camp & Associates; *m.* Mal Clason/TOM STACK & ASSOCIATES; *b.* Runk-Schoenberger/Grant Heilman Photography. 236: *t.* Larry Lefever/Grant Heilman Photography; *b.* Grant Heilman Photography. 237: *t.* Comstock/Michael Stuckey; *b.* © Susan McCartney-Photo Researchers, Inc. 238: G. Ziester/Peter Arnold, Inc. 239: Comstock/Michael Stuckey. 244: Courtesy of Kathy Griffin/Midwest Diving Specialist.

Unit 4 opener   253: David Madison.

Chapter 9   254–255: Ronald F. Thomas/Taurus Photos, Inc. 254: Michel Siffre/Sygma. 259: Light Mechanics for SBG; 264: *t.l.* © 1991 Sisse Brimberg/Woodfin Camp & Associates; *t.r.* Shelly Katz/Black Star; *b.l.* © Joseph Nettis/Photo Researchers, Inc. 266–267: Tom Walters/Tom Walters Photography. 268: © Ed Bock/The Stock Market. 269: Cheryl Griffin for SB&G; 272: © Richard Haynes for SBG.

Chapter 10   276–277: Barry Tenin. 280: *t.l.* Deneve Feigh Bunde/Unicorn Stock Photos. 282: Richard Haynes for SB&G. 283: Light Mechanics for SB&G. 284: *l.* Mark Tomalty/Masterfile; *r.* Bob Daemmrich. 285: *l.* Mitchell B. Reibel/Sportschrome/East/West. 286: Richard Benson/National Stock Network. 289, 296–298: *r.* Richard Haynes for SB&G. 299: Bob Daemmrich/The Image Works. 304: Kirby Harrison for SB&G.

ACKNOWLEDGMENTS

Grateful acknowledgment is made to the following publishers, authors, and agents for their permission to reprint copyrighted material. Any adaptations are noted in the individual acknowledgments and are made with the full knowledge and approval of the authors or their representatives. Every effort has been made to locate all copyright proprietors; any errors or omissions in copyright notices are inadvertent and will be corrected in future printings as they are discovered.

p. 110: "Dinosaurs" from *More Small Poems* by Valerie Worth. Copyright © 1976 by Valerie Worth. Reprinted by permission of Farrar, Straus and Giroux, Inc. Illustrations from *Dinosaurs: Poems Selected by Lee Bennett Hopkins* Copyright © 1978 by Murray Tinkelman, reprinted by permission of Harcourt Brace Jovanovich, Inc.

p. 112: "Fossils" from *Something New Begins* by Lilian Moore. Text: Copyright © 1982 by Lilian Moore. Reprinted with permission of Atheneum Publishers, an imprint of Macmillan Publishing Company. Illustrations from *Dinosaurs: Poems Selected by Lee Bennett Hopkins* Copyright © 1978 by Murray Tinkelman, reprinted by permission of Harcourt Brace Jovanovich, Inc.

p. 114: "What If..." by Isabel Joshlin Glaser. Used by permission of the author, who controls all rights. Illustrations from *Dinosaurs: Poems Selected by Lee Bennett Hopkins* Copyright © 1978 by Murray Tinkelman, reprinted by permission of Harcourt Brace Jovanovich, Inc.

pp. 168–174: "Balloons, Balloons!" from *The Big Balloon Race* by Eleanor Coerr, illustrated by Carolyn Croll. Text Copyright © 1981 by Eleanor Coerr. Illustrations Copyright © 1981 by Carolyn Croll. Reprinted by permission of Harper & Row, Publishers, Inc.

pp. 246–252: From *Storm in the Night* by Mary Stolz, illustrated by Pat Cummings. Text Copyright © 1988 by Mary Stolz. Illustrations Copyright © 1988 by Pat Cummings. Reprinted by permission of Harper & Row, Publishers, Inc., of the author, and of Roslyn Targ Literary Agency, Inc., New York.

pp. 306–312: From *The Bear's Bicycle* by Emilie Warren McLeod, illustrated by David McPhail. Text © 1975 by Emilie Warren McLeod. Illustrations © 1975 by David McPhail. By permission of Little, Brown & Company, Inc., and of André Deutsch Limited.